NORTON

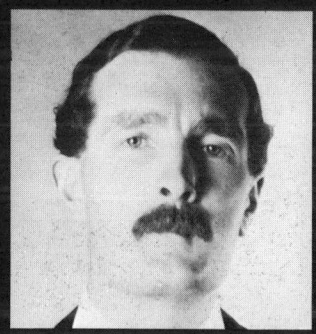

The Author
Dennis Howard

Dedicated to the cause of motorcycling, Dennis Howard was a member of the Editorial Staff of 'The Motor Cycle' until the early 1950s. Now a freelance, he specializes in the racing scene of the 'Golden Thirties' and is public relations officer of the racing section of the Vintage Motorcycle Club. He is an everyday rider of all types of motorcycle

Editorial team

Editor-in-Chief, Ballantine Illustrated History Books
Barrie Pitt

Editorial Director
David Mason

Art Director
Sarah Kingham

Consultant Editor
Prince Marshall

Cover Design : Michael Fry/Graham Bingham
Design : Michael Frost

Contents

Photographs and illustrations for this book have been selected from the following archives : Motorcycle ; Montagu Motor Museum ; Reynolds Tube Co. Ltd. ; Dennis Howard and Old Motor Magazine

Pride in success

This book makes great nostalgic reading. Even at the tender age of twelve the name Norton conjured up, in my young mind, a vision of the last word in motorcycles. And trips on the back of my brother's New Imperial to the Southport and Wallasey sand races, where Norton machines almost inevitably swept the board, added to my enthusiasm.

Little wonder that years later, after meeting Artie Bell, the Norton racing team number one, at the Scott trial in Yorkshire, an approach from Joe Craig, on Artie's recommendation, found me turning down an offer from AJS and hotfooting it to a meeting at the New Victoria Hotel in Birmingham, with the 'Professor' in person. This, of course, had nothing to do with road racing, only a contract to ride the new McCandless-inspired 500T in reliability trials. But I had far more in mind than that!

My place of work, the Norton factory at Bracebridge Street, was far from inspiring, either inside or out, and the machine shop across the road at R T Shelley's, with its hundreds of overhead pulleys and slapping belts, driving rather antiquated machinery, hardly spoke of grandeur. Yet the atmosphere was somehow 'electric', and this seemed to make itself felt by everyone in the place, not only in the racing and design departments, but from the works manager right down to the youngster who swept the floor. There was a feeling of pride to be working at Bracebridge Street.

I am convinced that this pride in the racing successes and in the name Norton itself produced more work per man hour, and unbelievable quality from the rather unsophisticated tools available, than could possibly have been achieved elsewhere in the industry.

This enthusiasm was evident on every occasion when I returned to the factory from my weekend trials or road races. My Monday morning progress from the factory entrance to the Competition Department, punctuated as it was every few yards by enquiries about the event, was slow to say the least.

My early road racing was confined to the 'garden gate' Manx Norton, but looking back, I realize how fortunate I was to become involved from the beginning of my professional racing career with the 'featherbed', a design which gave Nortons a new lease of life, and provided me with machines which so suited my particular riding style.

My two-and-a-half years with Nortons taught me a great deal, and the successes we achieved are, to this day, a great source of pride to me. Perhaps the most outstanding of those, the 1951 500cc Belgian Grand Prix, I consider to be my personal best, and worth recounting.

On the ultra fast Francorchamps circuit, we were really up against it, with a host of Italian multi-cylinder machines in opposition. However, a combination of many factors contributed to our ultimate success, not the least of these being a discussion on race tactics with Joe Craig during an evening stroll from our hotel down to Stavelot bend on the course.

Practice had shown that, unhindered by the poorer-handling Gilera, Guzzio and MVs, we could lap just as fast, and quite by chance the organisers had provided fuel for the race which, to date, was the best yet encountered. Joe had taken full advantage of this by raising the compression ratio of our engines to the limit of safety. Add to this the superb handling of the Norton, and we decided we were in with a chance, provided I could make the start of my life, build up sufficient lead during the comparatively twisty first mile or so before the Masta straight, and maintain that lead, no matter how slender, up the long climb with its occasional fast sweeping bends, leading to Francorchamps hairpin and the end of lap one, without being overtaken and involved in slipstreaming the faster Italian machines.

On the day this first lap lead was achieved with a few lengths to spare, and by riding on the limit of adhesion throughout the race, increasing our lead only by fractions of a second per lap, we made it, followed home by a Gilera, only seconds behind. Great, great Norton days!

Geoff Duke

THE EARLY YEARS

One of the earliest Nortons with
Clement engine, about 1902. The
model shown utilised a short
primary drive by chain

James Lansdowne Norton was destined to become one of the father figures in the world of motorcycle engineering. He was born in 1869, the son of a Birmingham cabinet maker, and as a boy obviously possessed an inherent engineering ability for it is known that he would construct model steam engines and present them in working order in the window of his home; so popular did these exhibitions become that the local constabulary were obliged to restrain the boy as the gathering crowds were, in official terms, likely to cause an obstruction. As a youth James Norton was apprenticed to a tool maker in the jewellery trade where the precision work involved could not have provided a better grounding for the young man. It was not long however before he had definite ideas about being in business on his own account and in the closing years

of the 19th century he had formed the Norton Manufacturing Company, making chains for the push cycles of the period and various other parts, the former undertaking being no small task alone.

The first Norton motor bicycle appeared during the year 1902, some eight years before the end of the Edwardian era. To describe the machine as a motor bicycle is correct, because an imported Belgian Clement engine was added to a more robust cycle frame, clipped to the front down tube, and a transmission consisting of a thin leather belt running from a pulley on the crankshaft to a suitable belt rim on the rear wheel. It is this machine that was the first to bear the Norton motif on its tank-side, although other machines had been built by Norton but not necessarily sold under his name.

There is no doubt that Norton was a very clever engineer, and was a founder member of the Institute of Automobile Engineers, and as a tribute to the man upon his early death in 1925 at the age of fifty-six, the Norton Scholarship in motorcycle engineering was introduced at Birmingham University. There has always been something about a Norton motorcycle that represents good honest solid workmanship, and by study of the machine as a whole it is obvious that true care in design and construction, and in consequence consideration for the owner-cum-rider has been the prime motive in manufacturing policy, thus giving an insight into the character of James Norton.

It is known that he was a deeply religious man, and a strong supporter of the Salvation Army, in fact there is a story that when Norton was brought before a Birmingham magistrate during the early years of this century for driving at excessive speed and for having made undue noise while testing one of his machines through the city, a plea was made that 'Mr Norton is not only a well respected motorcycle engineer, but also a leading light in

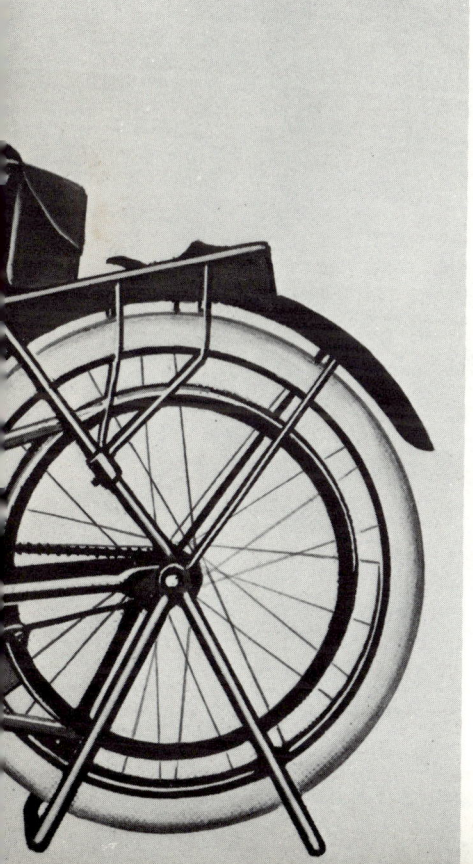

J. L. NORTON,
3½ NORTON

Salvation Army matters locally,' alas all was to no avail 'For Mr Norton is a motorcyclist and must be fined accordingly'. One may appreciate how the motorcyclist has been a persecuted soul from the very beginning.

There are happily those still with us who served their youthful years beneath the patriarchal wing of bearded James Norton and have described him as an intensely honest man with never an ill word for any soul; the expressions kindly and generous are also included in their appreciation, and a perfectionist in all of his ideals. As is the case with all men of high principle, anything tinged with other than the straight and narrow is abhorrent, and perhaps this is why Norton never enjoyed the greater financial rewards that could have been his; rather were motorcycles and motorcycling his life in the truest sense; and the satisfaction of knowing that purchasers of Norton machines were being provided with the ultimate in motorcycling pleasure.

This complete concern with ensuring that his motorcycle was the best that could be obtained led unfortunately to a situation in which the company came tragically near to liquidation, but was saved at the eleventh hour by a firm of engineers R T Shelley and Company who had formerly undertaken machining jobs for Norton; thus was formed Norton Motors Limited with premises at Samson Road North, in Birmingham.

A happy combination now existed for 'Pa' Norton, as he was affectionately referred to, for under the new organisation the engineering maestro could work away on his new designs while others with the necessary business acumen would attend to the company's financial affairs.

Previous mention of Norton's qualities would lead one to imagine that the man was also modest about his obvious abilities, and indeed the position

was such that any form of advertising had been of a very modest nature, sometimes merely a simple card advising potential purchasers that 'We have six models in stock to be cleared'. Under the completely revised company and most surely the Shelley influence, the motorcycles were now referred to as 'The Unapproachable Norton'. Two schools of thought exist as to how the Norton became 'Unapproachable' as a selling slogan, one declaring that following the first TT win by a Norton in 1907, plus various fastest times in hill climbs around this period, the marque was indeed rapidly becoming unapproachable. The arch-authority on motorcycle history C E Allen subscribes to the second school and considers that with the coming of the 1911 machine the slogan came into being. It must be explained that the TT winning machine and indeed certain other motorcycles constructed by Norton prior to 1911 were using twin cylinder Peugeot and other proprietory engines, and thus were not entirely Norton to the core.

To the dedicated vintage enthusiast, the most desirable models would be the BS (Brookland's Special) or BRS (Brookland's Road Special) both being classic examples of the early sporting Norton, details of which will naturally follow as the story progresses; these machines possessed however what is described in motorcycling circles as 'Thumping big single-cylinder side-valve engines with every power stroke representing a ton and a half of finest roast beef', and it is with such power units that Pa Norton was mostly associated. Many motorcycle historians have written in detail about the first TT race in 1907 and the various continental events that preceeded it and it is therefore not necessary to write yet again about the matter; it will be of interest however to note that from that very first Isle of Man race Norton machines have been represented in every TT meeting to date.

Early in 1907 first Secretary of the Auto Cycle Club Freddie Straight set about the pleasurable task of organising a race for machines not unsimilar to those on sale to the public, and with the great assistance of the Manx authorities it was decided that a short course in the Isle of Man would be most suitable. Two classes were to be catered for, namely single- and twin-cylinder machines, the only restriction being that fuel would be allocated on a ration basis: 90mpg for the singles and 75mpg for the twins. Efficient silencers had to be fitted, and pedalling gear was allowed to assist a flagging engine on the steeper parts of the course. The start and finish was at St Johns and riders were obliged to cover the sixteen-mile circuit ten times and each competitor had to make a compulsory ten-minute rest stop upon the completion of five laps, riders were dispatched at one-

A Peugeot engine similar to Rem Fowler's TT Norton. Only the exhaust valves were mechanically operated

minute intervals. Rembrandt Fowler, who died just a few years ago, was the winner of the twin-cylinder class and made the fastest lap at 42.91mph but not before he had repaired countless punctures, changed at least half a dozen sparking plugs and narrowly missed becoming a blazing inferno when he charged through a pack of fallen machines 'all well lit up'. The original telegram from the Isle of Man informing the Birmingham factory of Fowler's win read as follows 'Norton motor won easily. Record time. 44 ounces of petrol to spare. Fowler drove magnificently'. The winning machine was privately owned but had received some attention from James Norton; it weighed about 180 pounds and was powered by the French vee twin engine of 617cc. Automatic inlet valves were fitted, the 'tuning' amounted to increasing their light return spring pressure to about eight pounds.

The Norton possessed a very long wheelbase which was considered to

give superior road holding qualities and in proportion the frame was quite low leading some wags of the day to explain that this provided a shorter distance to fall in the event of a crash. All the braking the machine could boast was a stirrup type on the front wheel not unsimilar to those fitted to cycles of the period and the rear wheel relied upon the movement of a fibre shoe, operated by the rider's foot, acting upon the natural groove in the belt rim. 'Ixion' (Canon B H Davis of *The Motor Cycle*) maintained that a stout pair of hobnail boots served the purpose far more satisfactorily in retarding the forward progress of these early machines. It is said that the very first pit signal was made during this first TT race, for Pa Norton, having noticed that Fowler had not been operating the tank-top mounted hand oil-pump, the only system by which the motor received its vital lubrication, had written in bold letters on a suitably large card the word 'OIL' and had thrust it into the view of a doubtless sore and very tired Fowler to set about the necessary task.

Although much attention was given to the competitive aspect of the Norton's progress during these formative years it would appear that the 'Bread and Butter' machines were few and far between. However by 1909 no less than eight models were listed in the current Buyer's Guide ranging from two small models fitted with 2½hp JAP engines, and six with Norton engines of between 3½ and 5hp, prices ranging from thirty-six to seventy-two guineas. At this period magneto ignition became as standard a fitting as the Norton carburettor. The London Agents for Norton's machines were Harrods and Gamages. The old saying that 'Racing improves the breed' was obviously in

The Nortons, father and son, in the Isle of Man in 1912. James is seated on his favourite model, the Type Big 4

The imposing Brooklands Banking forms an excellent backcloth for O'Donovan astride 'Old Miracle'. The production power unit was undergoing test

the forefront of James Norton's mind, for he had raced his own models from 1909 until 1911 but retiring in the Isle of Man on all three occasions, he therefore decided not to take part himself in competitive sport again but to attend to the needs of other riders of his machines, however following the 1907 TT victory, and a ninth place in the following year (S C Perryman up) no Norton completed the course again until 1914 when two models were placed 46th and 51st respectively. The proving of a racing motorcycle is a long and tedious business and in all fairness Norton needed time to perfect his designs.

The scene was changing rapidly; no longer were classes divided into single- and twin-cylinder categories, now it was a matter of Junior and Senior capacities according to the cubic capacity of a machine. The full course in the 'Island' not so very different from that in use today was raced over, and in this the last sweet summer before the Kaiser War all the sporting young men stood beside their machines at Douglas topped with the new and compulsory safety helmet. Formerly riders had worn the dashing leather flying cap but following the death of Rudge rider Bateman when speeding over the Mountain section in 1913, the Auto Cycle Union as it was now called wisely insisted upon the necessary precaution. The war clouds were gathering but activity at Brooklands continued in a remarkably relaxed way and much testing of Norton machines took place there in the expert hands of the great D R O'Donovan. 'Don' was the brother-in-law of R T Shelley of Nortons and was considered somewhat of a wizard in his ability to extract quite phenomenal speeds from the side-valve engines. The system was that periodically a batch of newly finished engines would

Above: Participant in the All-Khaki races at Brooklands 1915. Pressure of business did not permit the continuation of such pleasantries. Above right and middle. On active service, 1917. Below: Norton rider 68 pushes off at Doncaster Speed Trials on Whit Monday 1914

The Public Schools Hill–Climb towards the end of the Great War, and Nortons are everywhere. W P Cubitt (Charterhouse), fastest time of the day on his 3½hp model

be sent down to Brooklands from the Birmingham factory and each one would be fitted into O'Donovan's mobile test bed and pounded round the three mile saucer until he was satisfied that the units were giving the required power and speed. Upon completion of a satisfactory test the engines were removed and duly returned to the Midlands where they would be installed in a production frame to await delivery to agent or customer. The mobile test bed possessed its own quite remarkable motor and had held many speed records at one time or other; affectionately known as 'Old Miracle' it must have first seen the light of day some tine in 1912. The side-valve Norton engine had the now classic dimensions of 79mm bore and 100mm stroke giving a capacity of 490cc and thus was a truly long-stroke unit. Fortunately 'Old Miracle' is still with us, having been owned by the late Graham Walker and now spending its autumn years in the Montagu Museum at Beaulieu. It is ridden in the annual Pioneer Run to Brighton in March and is still no mean performer. It is difficult to imagine that such a starkly simple machine, so very basic in appearance with its engine supported by the very lightest of frames, and direct belt drive to the rear wheel, had secured some 112 World and British records before the First World War, its top speed being then over 80mph. A move was made to new premises in 1916 when under contract to the Government Nortons were producing motorcycles for the Russian military forces as well as other pieces of equipment and the never-to-be-forgotten Bracebridge Street address came into being: but the time was four long years away when the bright young speedman of the 'Twenties would leap aboard his sporting BRS model.

19

ROAD TO SUCCESS

**The type of Norton that the author
Henry Williamson found the ideal
medium for his 'escape'**

Henry Williamson, the great naturalist and author of so many delightful books on the simple life, describes how, on returning from the First World War shattered and thoroughly disillusioned, he spent his savings and what gratuity he had earned on a single-speed Norton in 1920. Williamson gives splendid detail of his ride out of the steaming metropolis, along the quiet country roads, through sleepy West Country villages to his North Devon cottage retreat.

Presumably Henry Williamson's Norton was either a Brooklands Special or Brooklands Road Special; in either case, however, in his wallet would have been a certificate acting as a guarantee that the BS had attained a speed of 75mph over one kilometre at Brooklands, while had his model been the BRS then over the same distance the guaranteed speed would have been but five miles less. Although James Norton was providing in his immediate post war

programme the three-speed chain-drive 'Big Four' model (Norton's favourite and so named as its capacity of 633cc was then rated as four horse power) plus single- and three-speed versions of the TT model, the classic BS and BRS were much sought after pieces by 'Sporty Boy' particularly, and although in these the very earliest years of the 'Twenties the two belt drives were slightly obsolete they still enjoyed a remarkable following, no doubt due to their fine turn of speed. The BRS was often supplied with a simple device known as the Phillipson Pulley, although this proprietary fitting was readily adaptable to most single-speed belt-driven machines. The system provided a form of variable gear, for the pulley, mounted on the crankshaft outer end, had flanges that would close or open in relation to the engine revolutions, thus raising or lowering the gear according to the work the engine was obliged to undertake, indeed with a skilful rider aboard it was possible to keep the motor running when traffic was slow moving, while the pure single-speed man, clutchless, was for ever stopping and starting in town.

There appeared a charming little advertisement in a motor-cycling book of the 'Twenties, extolling the many virtues of the Phillipson Pulley which was presented thus: 'Hill-climbing with the World-famed Philipson Pulley'. 'Flexibility, Speed, Safety. Only two working parts, no other gear can compete in simplicity. Fitted to belt-driven machines by anyone in a few minutes. Price £8.8.0. Carriage Paid. A Gentleman writes us in' Wales ''It makes Mountaineering easy'' Send for illustrated booklet Phillipson and Co Ltd, Astley Bridge, Bolton, Lancs'.

The classic TT races were resumed in 1920 with Nortons entered in the Senior event (500cc) and following some spirited riding by Douggie Brown on the new three-speed chain-driven model, still with the old side-valve engine however, he secured second place behind the Sunbeam of Tommy de

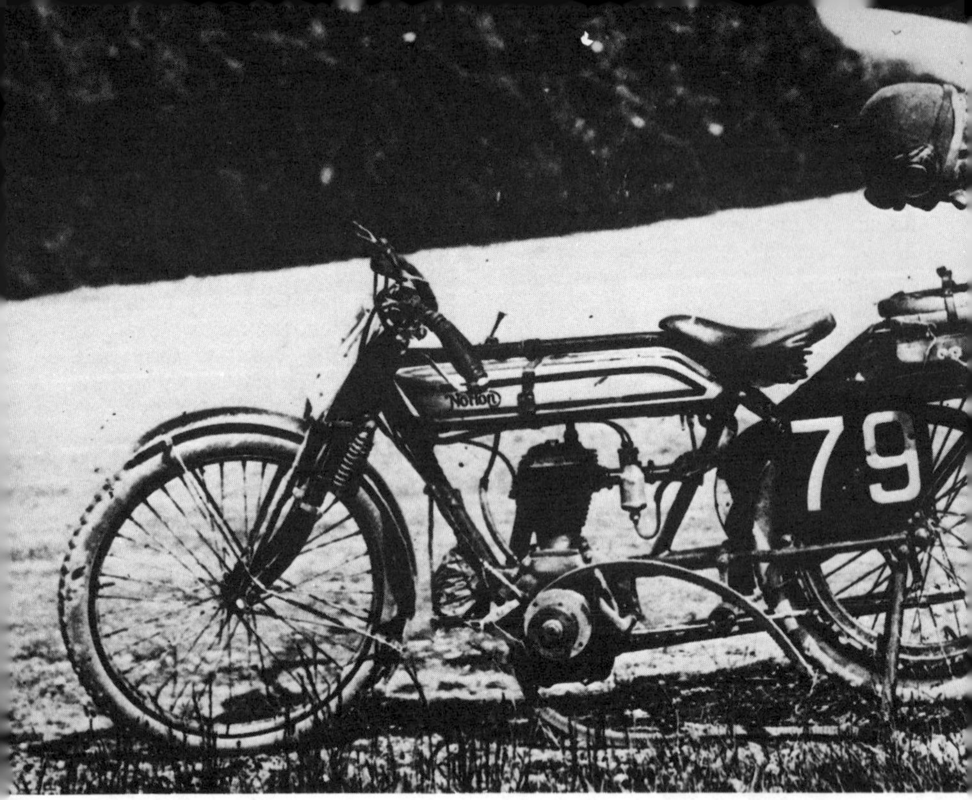
Norton
79

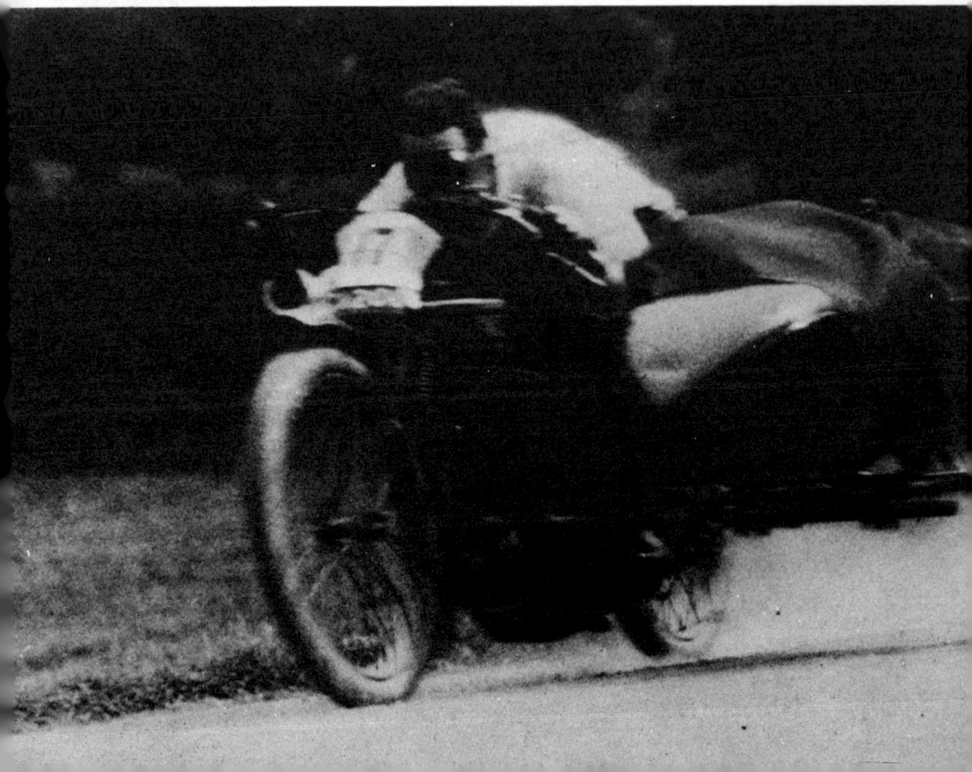

The last belt-driven machine to finish a TT race: Norman Black repairs a puncture. This famous Norton is now owned and used by John Moore of Reading

la Hay. Perhaps the most outstanding performance was to the credit of amateur rider Norman Black who had pluckily entered on a standard belt driven Norton. His chief troubles were punctures and belt stops, the latter being due to oil leakages. On taking out his back wheel to change a tube on the last lap he found the bearings were completely chewed up and rode thirty miles with no balls whatsoever in the rear hub. Even so he finished in a very creditable eleventh position and in so doing became the rider of the last belt-driven machine to finish a TT race. Out of thirteen Nortons entered for this the first post-war TT, five were to retire and the remainder to finish in second (Brown), fourth, seventh, eighth, tenth, eleventh (Black), thirteenth and fourteenth positions.

The new racing Norton as described not only boasted a three-speed gearbox and final drive by chain but also a hand-cum-stick gear-change, for from a small plate mounted above the gearbox a long lever (usually positioned at about two o'clock) was attached. Selection of a gear was made by raising or lowering this lever according to whether the rider wished to change up or down. Many diehards on very principle still operated the lever by hand, but at racing speeds it now took a fairly brave man to remove his hand from the handlebars to execute a change, and a nicely judged kick seemed to work much better.

For 1921 the racing machines were very little changed but certain minor improvements were made; the wheelbase was shortened to $56\frac{1}{2}$ inches, the oil pump was foot-operated and the saddle height was lowered. An experi-

Victor Horsman puts a TT Norton through its paces at Chatsworth Speed Trials

ment using aluminium pistons was tried but at this stage they did not prove entirely satisfactory and a reversion to the old cast iron ones was made until the difficulties could be attended to. The TT models were certainly fast enough to win but did not shine at all with the highest placed machine in sixth position. A more encouraging state of affairs existed at Brooklands however when 'Wizard' O'Donovan in company with Victor Horsman and the late Rex Judd went out to attempt the double twelve hour record. What exactly was the double twelve? Unlike the rather free license afforded record seekers on the Continent who could bat on all through the night if they were so disposed, the near residents of Weybridge managed to obtain an order restricting any form

The French Grand Prix of 1921. Hubert Hassall makes adjustments to his racing Norton

of night-riding at Brooklands. What would normally have been referred to as a twenty-four hour attempt therefore was divided into two stages of twelve hours duration each. It would appear that Rex Judd was by far the most robust rider for where Horsman and O'Donovan were well and truly fagged after the first twelve hours, Judd rode for nearly the whole of the second twelve-hour period and in so doing took the record at 60.7mph, the Norton running smoothly at the scheduled speed of just over 60mph. In addition to these solo motorcycle attempts Judd was of course by reason of his light weight and small stature an ideal passenger for both sidecar races and record attempts, and his brilliance on Douglas machines at a slightly later period was the talk of the Brooklands 'Regulars'.

Only a few days before Rex Judd died he was in good voice reminiscing about the great times at Brooklands, and by

chance C E Allen was fortunate to be at his bedside. He asked Judd what was the secret behind the preparation of the fast Nortons. The answer was a surprisingly simple one, apparently there were no highly scientific tuning methods, just a lot of elbow grease in polishing the internals and setting accurately the transmission line, getting the timing and carburation spot-on and running in the engines until they were really free. There are several very fine photographs of the 1921 record breaking Norton at Brooklands with what appears to be a very adequate binding of brown paper around the hand-cum-foot operated gear change lever; it was not uncommon for machines raced at Brooklands to be padded where any aid to comfort was readily accepted in preference to being pounded to near pulp following a 200-mile race, but in this particular case it was to satisfy a slight fussiness in James Norton's character. A very close friend of Rex Judd, and a man who participated in these attempts at Brooklands in one way or other is Bill Fruin of Benson in Oxfordshire, possibly the greatest restorer of early Nortons. Questioned about the brown paper Fruin replied 'You know Pa Norton was a fussy old bastard, although I hasten to add we all loved and respected him dearly, but he did carry on about protecting all plated parts, and as much attention had to be paid in ensuring that that ruddy brown paper was kept in position on the gear lever as getting down to the more serious work of testing and record breaking'

Some idea of the far sightedness of James Norton may be gained from the fact that as early as 1913 he had talked not only of overhead-valve engines but

A unique pair : D R O'Donovan and a youthful Rex Judd at Brooklands

The experimental overhead–valve engine that made its first and subsequent sensational appearances at Brooklands. The small coil springs were fitted to provide the double function of 'disciplining' both the rockers and push rods even of desmodromic valve gear (mechanical return of the valves to their closed position) and speeds of his racing machines that would be between 120 and 150mph as being possible at a not too great distance in the future, all of which materialised in due course. By 1922 an experimental pushrod operated overhead-valve Norton engine was sent down to Brooklands for development and although O'Donovan was as usual to be involved deeply in the experimental work it appears he was not particularly impressed by the new unit at first and procrastinated over getting it into a suitable frame. This was the period of the individual and no doubt Pa Norton, who respected, while not necessarily agreeing with, O'Donovan's attitude, allowed him to take his time. At last a complete machine was built for testing however, and on its first outing promptly attained a speed of 98mph, some four miles an hour faster than was possible with the very best side-valve models. The new design retained the bore and stroke dimensions of the side-valve unit (79 by 100mm – 490cc) and the cycle parts followed normal practice although the stirrup front brake had been replaced by one of the internal expanding type, giving at this time just a little more efficiency. Rex Judd, as previously mentioned, now about to conclude Norton testing for Douglas, Bert Denly, a local butcher, joined O'Donovan to continue the experimental and record-breaking work. In later years Denly transferred his attention to racing cars and was involved in some remarkably courageous feats in this new sphere.

Whereas the modern 'Grand Prix' type of racing motorcycle bears little resemblance to the 'as ridden on the road' machine, in the early years of the motorcycle industry it was quite possible to purchase a model that possessed all the necessary refinements for road racing, in fact a correct policy if the Tourist Trophy races were to be taken seriously, and indeed one that James Norton strongly adhered to.

Nearly all his machines raced in the 1922 races were virtually standard catalogue models with an only slight exterior difference; they had a separate oil tank affixed to the saddle tube.

Several of the new overhead-valve models were entered alongside the older side-valve jobs, but only one actually started in the race, and rather ironically showed little or no superiority over the latter, in fact it retired on the sixth lap. Regardless of this failure, which was not due to any major fault in the design, serious production went ahead and thus came into being the now famous Model 18. A handsome machine finished in the traditional Norton black and silver with all the usual bright parts nickel plated. The petrol tank was a beautiful example of the craftsman's art: from sheet steel, the top, bottom and sides were formed as separate pieces and then soldered into place, the scolloped bottom edge not only serving to give pleasure to the eye but fulfilling the more practical purpose of preventing splitting. As a woman's hair is her crowning glory, so the proud Norton owner would regard his petrol tank, in fact many went to the extent of sporting an all-nickel-plated affair.

Before 1922 was out the new overhead-valve Norton had raised the world's flying kilometre (500cc Class) to 89.22mph and more than satisfied the demands of the high-speed sporting rider, and was undoubtedly the fleetest standard single-cylinder machine of its day.

The Maudes Trophy, a special award made to motorcycle manufacturers for some particularly testing feat was introduced in 1923 and James Norton decided to compete for the award, for by winning 'the Maudes' Norton's prestige would be boosted to even greater heights, and the man in the street would know he was getting value for his money.

A machine was assembled from a selection of standard parts under the ever vigilant eye of an ACU observer. Without any specialised preparation

Above : Rex Judd astride the new
OHV job. Above right : Manx
youngsters show interest in Norton
activities during the 1922 TT. Below :
Tough roads, tough men : George
Tucker and passenger W Moore win
the 1923 Belgian Sidecar Grand Prix
on a model which was the immediate
forerunner of the 588cc Model 19

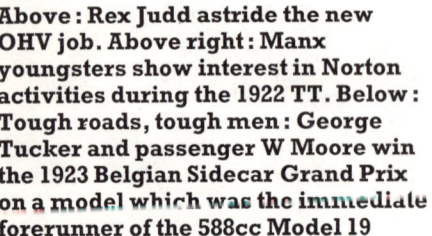

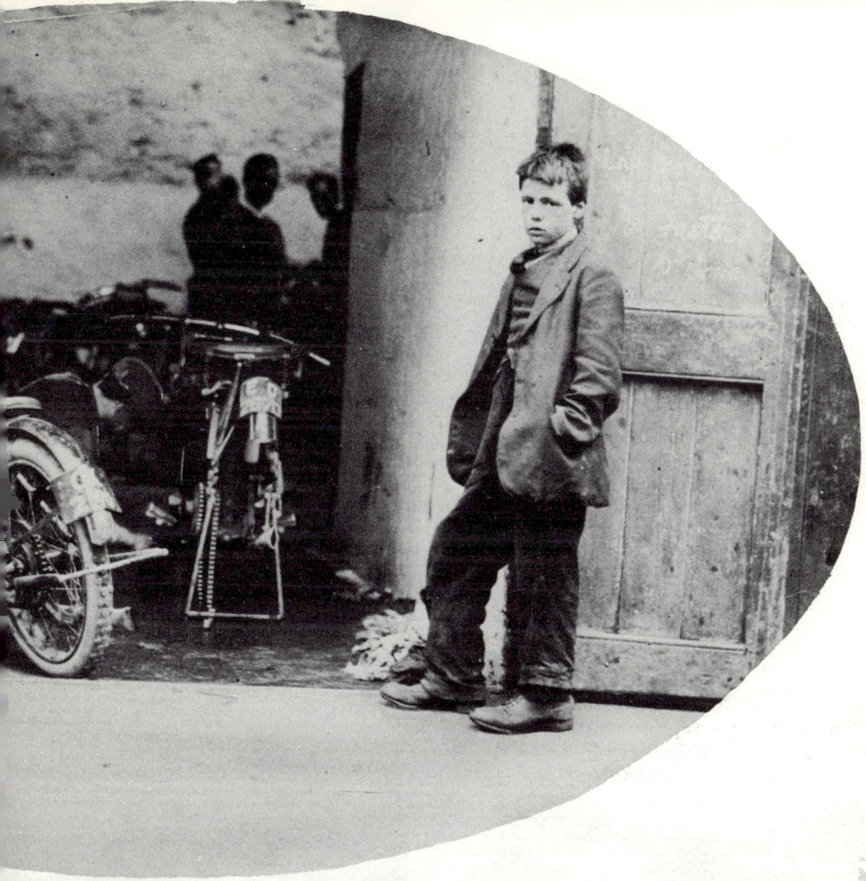

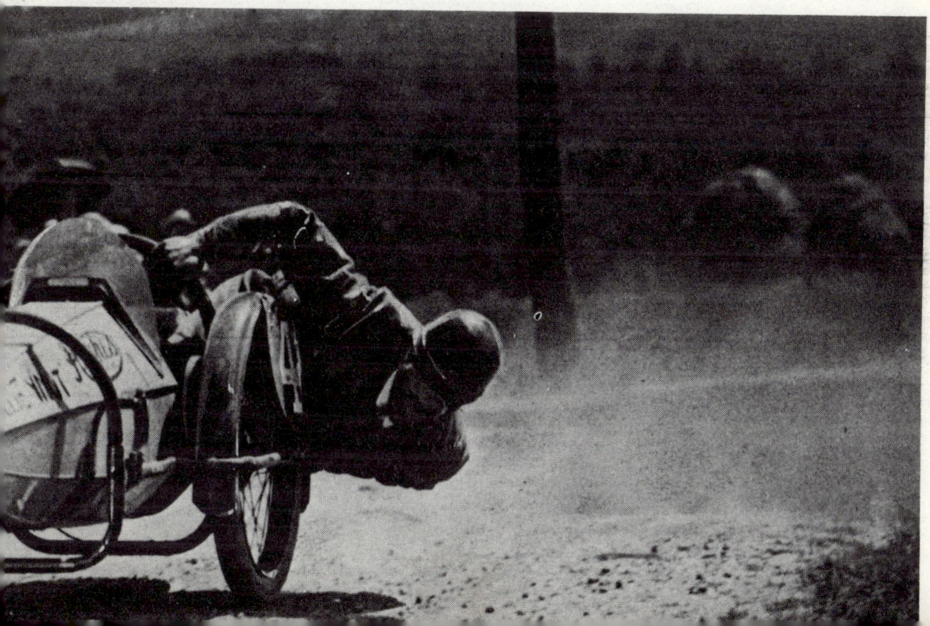

the Norton, ridden by a team consisting of O'Donovan, Denly and Nigel Spring (later to be associated with the racing Velocettes) promptly proceeded to smash no fewer than eighteen world records at Brooklands. 'Enough' cried the ACU and the trophy was Nortons' and indeed remained so for a further three years. For 1923 all the works-entered Nortons in the TT were fitted with the now tried and proved overhead-valve engines, and with the recent introduction of a 600cc Sidecar class certain models had their stroke increased by a further 20mm thus giving a capacity of 588cc. Graham Black finished second in the Senior race to Manxman Tom Sheard's Douglas, with other Nortons filling fourth, fifth, seventh and fourteenth places. Additionally the late and sadly missed Graham Walker with passenger Tommy Mahon took second place

Olympia Motor Cycle Show in the early 1920s. Amid the ferns and potted plants several Nortons can be seen at the bottom left of the picture

in the Sidecar event, the famous TT Hughes sidecar being named as 'Willy Stikkit'. Graham Walker had commenced his competition career in the immediate post-war years, had excelled as a sprinter on the old side-valvers and was already a likely force to be reckoned with in the 'Island'. He had been works manager at one time with considerable influence on the developement side at Nortons and in 1938 became Editor of *Motor Cycling* following a very successful life at speed on two wheels. Graham Walker was undoubtedly the BBC's finest commentator when covering the TT races; he passed away, when in semi-retirement he had accepted the post of curator of the motorcycle section at Beaulieu Musuem.

It should not be imagined that the utility rider was at all neglected during these formative years, for in strict accordance with Norton policy all refinements and any constructional changes made on the competition models were usually listed, where appropriate, in the catalogue for the

following year's machines, thus an intended purchaser of a Norton who visited the Motor Cycle Show at Olympia in 1923, would enjoy the benefit of the year's racing and consequential development in his 1924 mount.

Already the side-valve models 16H and 'Big Four' were giving yeoman service for the heavy work, particularly when a side-car was attached. Now in addition to the overhead-valve Model 18 came the 19 with its 588cc engine, in fact an enlarged version of the former. The enthusiastic motorcyclist may be described as a very ingenious bird, and one such example must surely be Peter Waring, former driver of the Grand Prix Lago Talbot cars, who is always ready to wax eloquent over his experiences in the 'Twenties with various Nortons. Waring tells of the dodge by which one could raise the compression ratio of a Model 19 by fitting a piston from the smaller model. Being of the same bore dimensions the pistons from either machine were inter-changeable, the 19 however had

a concave crown piston of the lower compression type (for hard slogging) and Waring required real performance at the top end of the scale; thus a Model 18 piston with its slightly domed crown was fitted, and according to Waring this raised the compression ratio of the larger machine by one to one and a half. On the low-octane fuels of the period Waring's Norton was a real flyer nevertheless, as a result of this little piece of surgery.

It is understood that Pa Norton was not a particularly demonstrative man, but by now he must have enjoyed a quiet satisfaction in the knowledge that his motorcycles were reaping their just rewards. On the Continent H W Hassall and J W Hollowell had gained second and third places in the French Grand Prix, then the most important event after the TT races, while Bert Denly crossed the finishing line as victor of the 200 mile solo race at Brooklands on his 500cc Norton, and

The type of Norton that underwent Peter Waring's surgery

made many successful attacks on the half-litre hour record, and by raising it to 82.67mph in June 1923 made it the first occasion on which the classic hour record had exceeded eighty miles per hour. In Ireland, the immortal Joe Craig won the 600cc class of the Ulster Grand Prix: the mighty 'Joe' – the man who was soon to play such a dramatic role in Norton racing development.

To the younger inhabitants of our large cities nowadays it would be difficult to imagine just how many Nortons were to be seen going about their various duties during the third

Great things yet to come: Joe Craig in 1924, during his early days, and a regular winner of the Ulster Grand Prix 600cc class. Webb forks have been fitted to his machine

decade of this century. The window cleaner would invariably ride a Norton Model 16H or Big Four with side float onto which would be attached his ladders and other equipment. Having come into contact with a number of now retired musicians, mostly fiddle players, it seems that the Norton was a sure favourite for complete reliability where engagements ranged from Bournemouth to Scarborough. With their instruments securely fastened to the carrier, these men checked that there was sufficient water and carbide in their lighting sets, donned a pair of Hutchinson waders, slipped on their waterproof Ponchos, and with flying helmet and goggles in place, set forth along the Great North Road. Here again Peter Waring, not only a suitable 'Doctor' for obtaining the best results from his Model 19, was also a keen

amateur competition dancer in the 'Twenties and describes how he could remain completely immaculate in white tie and tails beneath his riding equipment regardless of the frightening experience he was bound to suffer, particularly in wet weather, when the combination of tramlines and a road surface composed of wood sets would bring the best man down at some time or other.

It is unusual to associate the Norton marque with other than large capacity mounts, but in 1924 experiments were being conducted on a 250cc model, possibly with a view to entering the Lightweight class of the TT. The smaller Norton bore a basic similarity to the 500cc jobs and the overhead-valve arrangement was incorporated into the design. The bore and stroke were 63mm and 80mm respectively and the pushrod-operated valves were set at 90 degrees, and a detachable cylinder head was fitted. Into the light alloy piston were fitted two piston rings sharing the same groove, larger than usual. Full mechanical lubrication was employed, and there were internal expanding brakes on both wheels. It is regrettable that nothing appears to have come of this interesting quarter-litre model due no doubt to the fact that the company already found it hard to satisfy the demand for their existing range of machines, and the single cylinder 250 was 'spiked' for all time. With an estimated speed of seventy

Maudes Trophy winners again, before leaving Land's End: the outfit looks remarkably healthy. Phil Pike is at the helm with Arthur Bourne in the sidecar

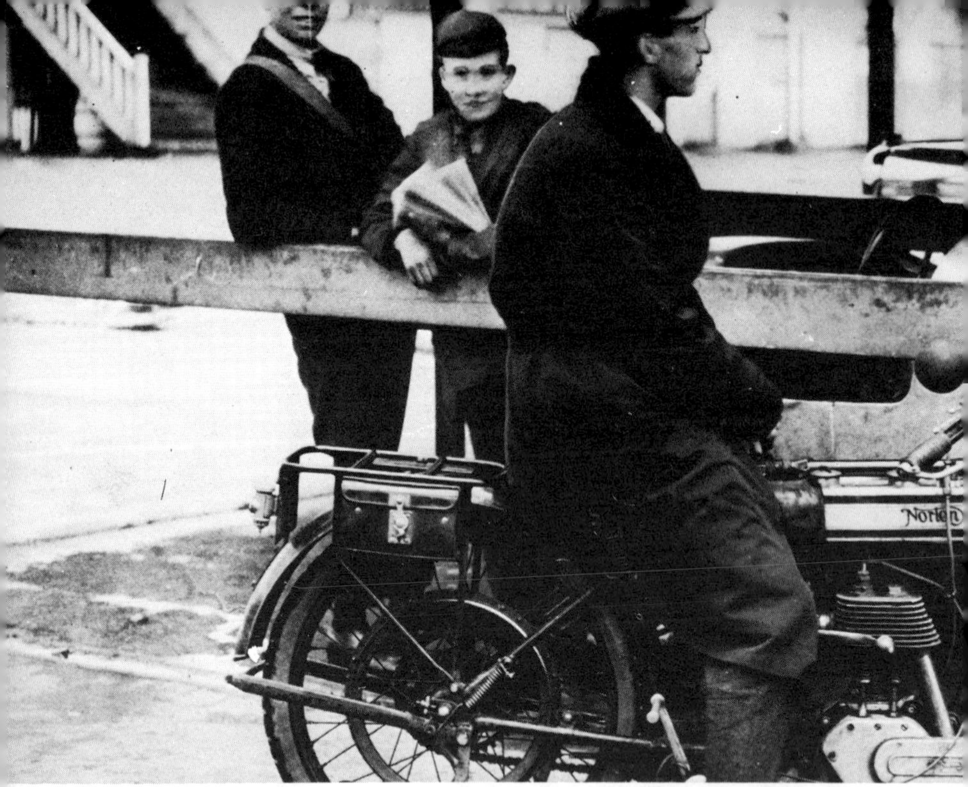
Norton

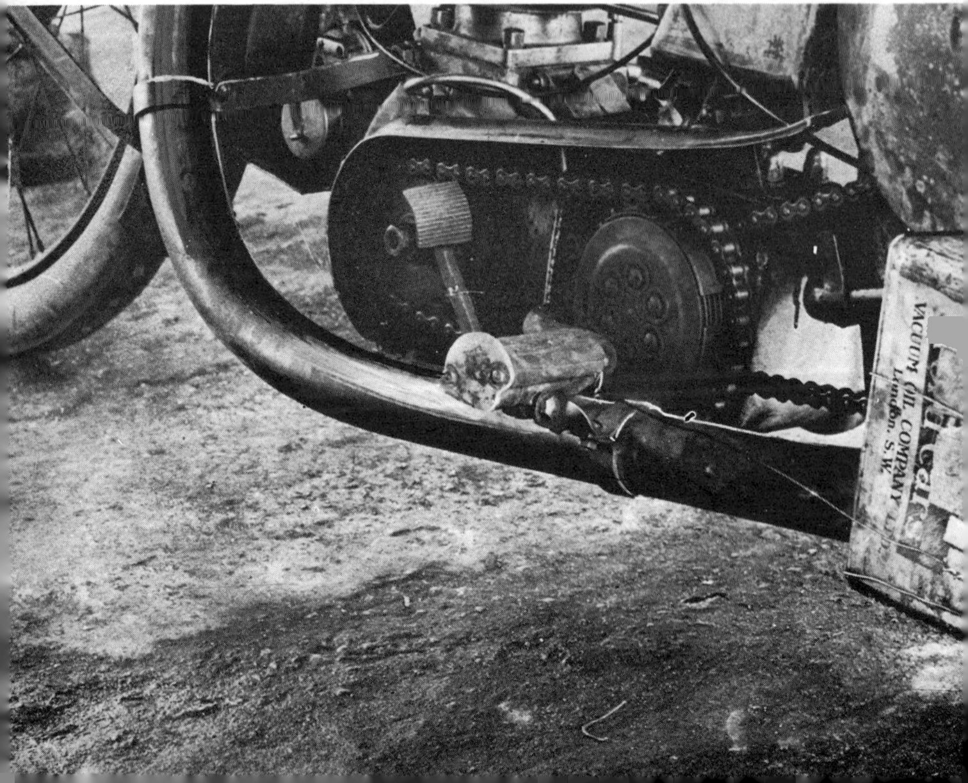
VACUUM OIL COMPANY
London. S.W.

miles per hour such a Norton might well have altered British fortunes in the Lightweight classes for some years, and it is interesting to ponder on when and if the Continental dominance of 250cc racing would have come in consequence.

By the time TT week had finished in June 1924, ex-Royal Flying Corps pilot Alec Bennett had brought his Norton home in first place in the Senior race at 61.64mph – the first time the event had been won at over 60mph. George Tucker had meanwhile kept the Norton banner flying by securing victory in the Sidecar race at over 50mph; to quote a modern phrase 'It was all happening'. The dear old Maudes Trophy was again to go to a machine from Bracebridge Street after a gruelling run from Land's End to John O' Groats, four times no less, at a speed schedule of 20mph. This was not all however, for there followed twenty ascents of Porlock Hill in Somerset by the 633cc Big Four and sidecar. The outfit was built from standard parts selected by Auto Cycle Union engineer Arthur Bourne ('Torrens' of *The Motor Cycle*, at a later date) and completed the first part of the test without trouble, but while on the way to Porlock the device was crushed against a wall when in collision with a tourist coach, and required quite extensive repairs. Still under supervision, the motorcycle and sidecar were straightened out, with the assistance and facilities of a local Norton Agent and the final part of the test was completed without further incident. Knowing only too well the 'characters' who participated in these remarkable stunts it is not difficult to picture the scene, a hilarious combination of tea by the gallon, cigarettes held by very oily fingers, good-natured banter mixed with a full quota of nicely selected words.

The cure : Lowe's Norton with Vacuum Oil can silencer

A NEW ERA

The governor: a picture taken a
short time before his death

In April 1925 James Norton passed away. He has been suffering from what was described as an incurable illness and had in fact willed himself to remain alive for about three years longer than his doctors had given him. Such had been the state of his health in 1924 that he was ordered to take a long holiday which was duly spent in South Africa. This was the second occasion on which he had visited the country for in 1921 accompanied by his sister-in-law he had taken his favourite model Big Four and sidecar on a world tour with the object of studying overseas conditions first-hand in order that future export models could be adapted to suit colonial going where appropriate. An outcome of this tour had been the raising of the ground clearance on most export machines to five inches, but this was only one of many alterations made by Norton to these models.

With his death one of the best loved and respected pioneers of the motorcycle industry passed from the scene. Affectionate reference to Norton as the 'Old Man' or Pa is interesting for he was only in his mid-fifties, but his general manner and patriarchal attitude plus his silver bearded appearance and traditional pince-nez gave him looks that were more associated with gentlemen in their very senior years. If one recalls to mind an ageing Bernard Shaw, complete with those celebrated Norfolk jackets, knickerbockers and tall stockings, one will have some idea of Norton's physical appearance. Fortunately those that had served under Norton were made of similar fibre and the motorcycle programme went forward in a manner that would not have disturbed 'the Governor'.

It is a little ironic perhaps that in the very year of Norton's death, the company that he had started approached its long road of fame with machines that proudly bore his name winning the Swiss, Russian, Polish and Italian road racing championships, in addition to the Dutch, Danish and Hungarian TT races and the Ulster and Belgian Grands Prix. In the Amateur TT, a September meeting held on the famous course in the Isle of Man, Nortons occupied first, second and third places, the winner, Sub-Lieutenant H G Dobbs RN, completing the course in just over three hours at a speed of 59.97mph. Three months earlier in the International TT event Alec Bennett had worked hard to gain a third place in the Senior race against the tough opposition of Howard Davies on his new and very potent HRD machine, while the Norton pair A E Taylor and George Grinton brought their Model 19s home second and third respectively in the 151 mile sidecar race.

On the Continent the great Tazio Nuvolari, later to be one of the select few to tame the rear-engined Auto-Union Grand Prix cars, was serving his apprenticeship on overhead-valve Nortons by winning various local Italian races including the Circuit de Cremona. Unlike the present day system, where it is possible to count the number of Grand Prix drivers who served their novitiate as motorcycle champions on the fingers of one hand, it was almost an unwritten rule that two wheels had to be mastered before four. Already rival motorcycle manufacturers could be justifiably envious of the supremacy that Norton machines had built up for themselves and in this respect it is necessary to refer to the Maudes Trophy yet again, indeed it seemed that the handsome cup would remain at Bracebridge Street permanently. For the 1925 attempt a 588cc Model 19 and sidecar, and a 490cc machine in solo form were chosen and assembled under the familiar ACU supervision. For the road section of the test a route embracing the courses of the 'Exeter Trial', 'Lands End', 'The Edinburgh' and 'John O' Groats' were used, being a total distance of 3,183 miles. The speed schedule was 20mph. Upon conclusion of this severe trial a speed test was undertaken at Brooklands following routine maintenance and a decoke of each machine. Records were then attacked and secured, many

Above: Glencrutchery Road line-up for the 1925 Senior TT. Alec Bennett's Norton is shown fitted with the braced forks, primarily intended for sidecar use. Rex Judd enjoys the last cigarette for nearly four hours. Above right: A very sporting set-up: the sons of the President of Hungary with their Model 19 and Torpedo sidecar in 1925. Below: TT editions of The Motor Cycle are assembled for flight to the Isle of Man

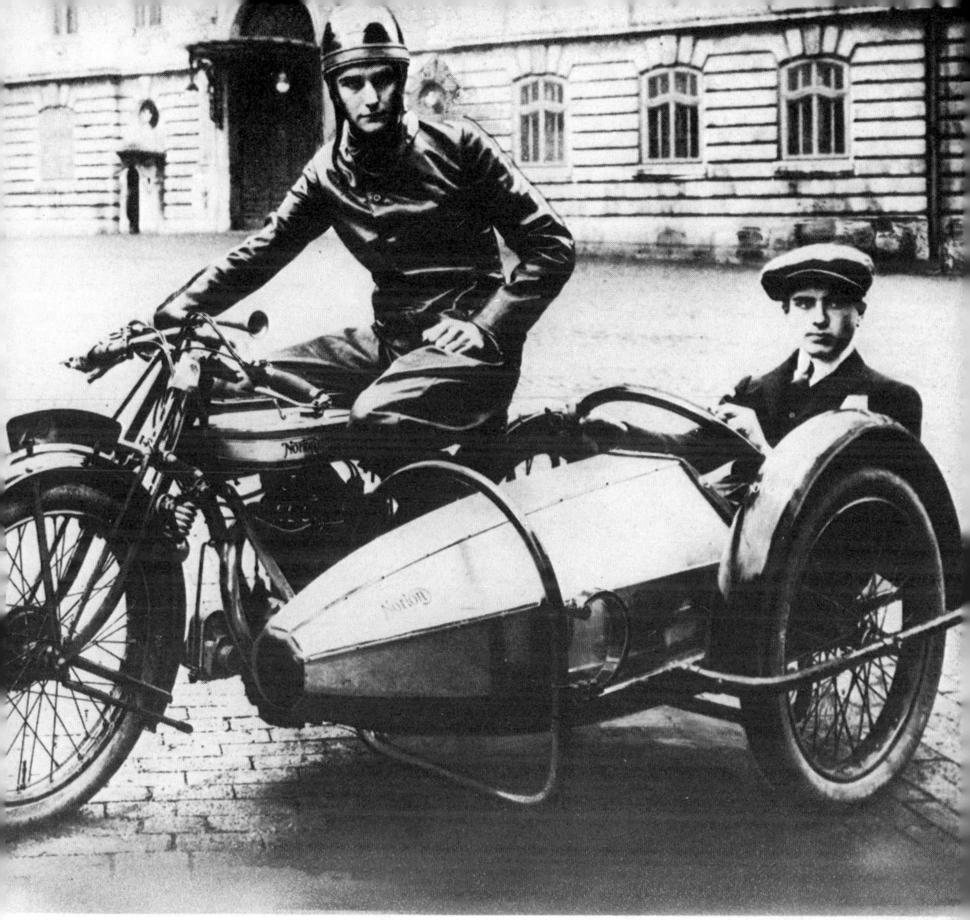
Norton
Norton

MOTOR CYCLE
SPECIAL
AEROPLANE
EDITION
MOTOR CYCLE
SPECIAL
AEROPLANE
EDITION

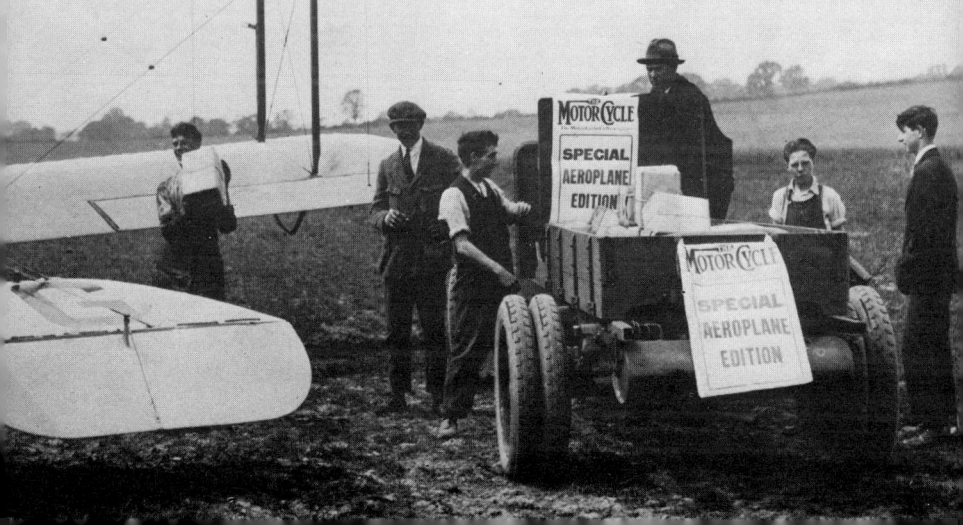

from the 500 miles upwards and the ten, eleven and twelve hour records. On a fourth Maudes attempt in the following year another demanding test was completed which included one hundred climbs of Bwlch-y-Groes in North Wales by a Model 19 and sidecar plus a 1,500 mile road test over the Land's End to John O' Groats route. The operations conducted and the miles consumed are inclined to induce verbal dyspepsia. Until very recent years no TT rider had matched the number of 'Island' victories attained by the great Stanley Woods whose road racing career started in 1922 and finished seventeen years later, in 1939. Stanley's father was a representative for Mackintosh's the toffee people and visited retailers in his native Ireland on a large Harley Davidson outfit. Possessing all the confidence and charm associated with folk from 'across the water', Woods Junior persuaded Senior that an ideal working arrangement would be for the boy to attend to all chauffeuring duties on the Harley while his father need attend solely to the requirements of his many customers. It appears the plan was accepted although whether Mr Woods, the father, knew that from time to time the motorcycle would be unhitched from its commercial sidecar to be ridden in local speed trials is not known but the outcome of this taste for fast motorcycle competition work brought Stanley 'Works' rides in due course, on a variety of machines and the start of a really professional road-racing career on Nortons in 1926. In this the first year of Wood's association with Bracebridge Street a good omen was sounded, for he won the Senior TT at 67.54mph although conceding fastest lap to the maker and breaker of TT lap records Jimmy Simpson who was then riding for AJS.

The TT Nortons were not unlike

Two great Brooklands men. Left: Chris Staniland with outfit; Staniland was later to become Chief Test Pilot for Fairey Aviation. Far right: Pat Driscoll, with an additional fuel supply on top of the standard tank. Below: The solid coach-built twin-seat Norton sidecar

those raced the previous year in certain respects but the flat petrol tank that had nestled so comfortably between the top tubes of the frame had been discarded in place of pannier tanks, one on each side of the tank tubes with suitable packing between the two units, contrary to the widely accepted notion that this was the introduction of the first saddle tanks on the racing Nortons. What was important however was the fact that more petrol could be carried with the new design.

The rather antiquated dummy belt-rim rear-brake system was abandoned in favour of the considerably more efficient internal expanding drum assembly, and, but for a few other very minor detail changes, that was that.

When the show models made their appearance in London in the winter of 1926 four-speed gearboxes were available on the Big Four and Model 19 road machines, along with other overhead-valve jobs being fitted with separate oil tanks, so following TT practice. Front-brake diameters were increased to seven inches and a system of automatic lubrication to the primary-drive chain was incorporated, the modifications also applying to the other side-valve model in the range; the 16H. On machines fitted with the new four-speed gear boxes a cross-

over final-drive was used, thus instead of the mainshaft mounted sprocket being in its former position, inboard of the clutch assembly, it was now situated, running on a counter shaft, on the machine's off-side. Having satisfied themselves that the sporting and utility riders were well catered for, at least for another year, the company turned their attention to devising better systems of engine efficiency, the result of which became yet another remarkable turning-point in Norton history. Already the brains at Bracebridge Street considered that the pushrod-operated overhead-valve engine had its limitations, at least as far as high speed racing work was involved, and one cannot help feeling that had James Norton been spared from higher duties for just a few more years both his thinking and subsequent action would have been entirely in mesh with the policy that the company was now to

adopt. Now forty-five years on from those exciting early months of 1927 the introduction of the overhead camshaft engine by Nortons appears in retrospect all so logical and indeed satisfying. Where other· manufacturers admittedly had bold new designs on the stocks, their accountants held supreme power and thwarted moves where the heavy but necessary expenses of racing development were required, and the consequential shelving of potential 'winners'. In contrast to these frustrated firms, Nortons ploughed on in their sure-footed way prepared to offer an honest explanation for any failure, if indeed any existed. No doubt in the fertile engineering mind of Pa Norton thoughts of camshaft

The first appearance of the large tank made up in two halves

engines had existed a long time before but it was left to Walter Moore to design and, to a degree, supervise the development of the first new engine. In place of pushrods, which in turn actuated rockers, one to each valve, on the earlier design, a vertical shaft was driven from a set of bevel gears housed in a smooth 'blister' on the off-side crankcase half. Bolted to the cylinder head was an alloy cambox which in turn contained the camshaft and its own set of bevels. From the two camshaft lobes, short pivoted rockers were pressed onto the tips of the valve stems at an appropriate time in relation to the four-stroke cycle of operation, the inlet and exhaust valves returning to their closed position by the expansion of a coiled spring suitably housed in each case.

Both pushrod and overhead cam-

STANLEY WOODS immediately after winning the 1926 Senior T.T. on a *Norton*

shaft models were ridden in the TT alongside each other, the strategy being no doubt that should the newer design experience teething troubles, the older versions might take over. It would be well to bear in mind that the older models were still to enjoy their moments of success in other spheres of motorcycle competition for many years to come.

All was set for Stanley Woods to bring off his second Norton victory. With the new model, he had already made fastest lap at over 70mph in this his fourth Senior TT but was to retire on his fifth circuit with clutch trouble. Woods of course should have won, because on the first second and third laps he was leading the second man Bennett by an ever increasing number of seconds per lap, but was not aware until after the race as to the extent of these time margins. After four laps Woods came in to refuel, his only pit instructions being that he was in the lead and should maintain his present pace. Alas, the pace played havoc with his clutch and brought about the retirement with only two laps to go and a lead on time of five minutes. One can imagine how Stanley must have felt. However the experience formed the basis of his 'secret' signalling stations around the course in future years and no doubt contributed to his many nicely judged victories. Although yielding victory to team mate Alec Bennett on a sister machine, Woods, with an overhead camshaft engine, went on to win the Belgian, Dutch and Swiss Grands

Delightful sporting gear for the Inter-Varsity Hill Climb at Henley Park in March 1926

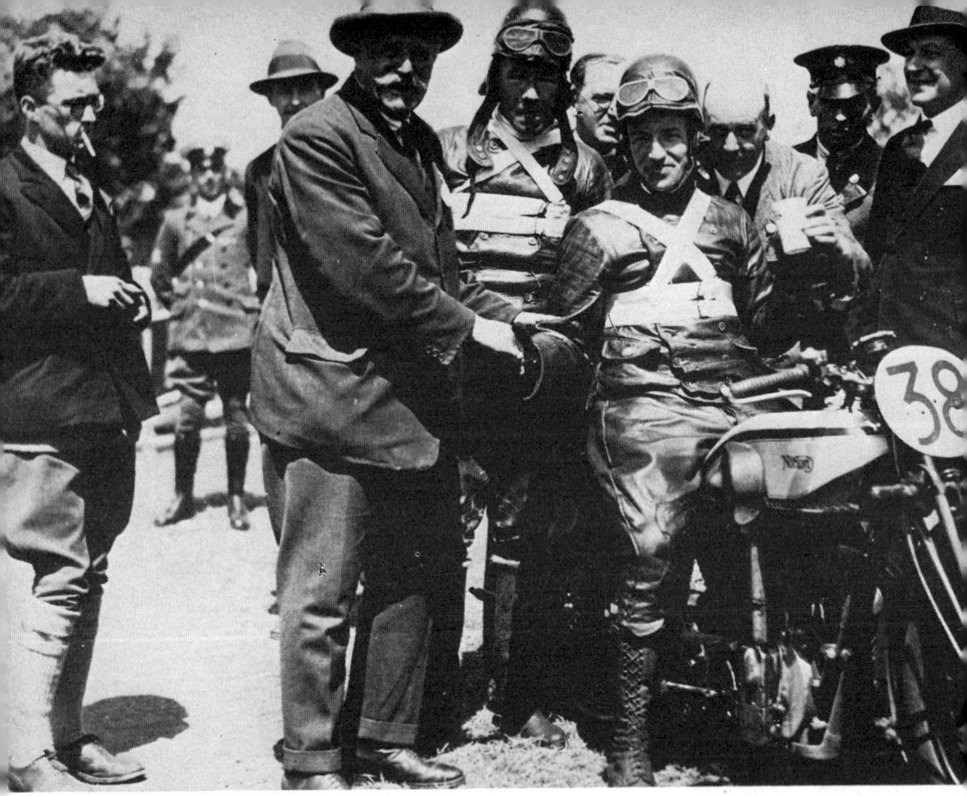
38
Norton

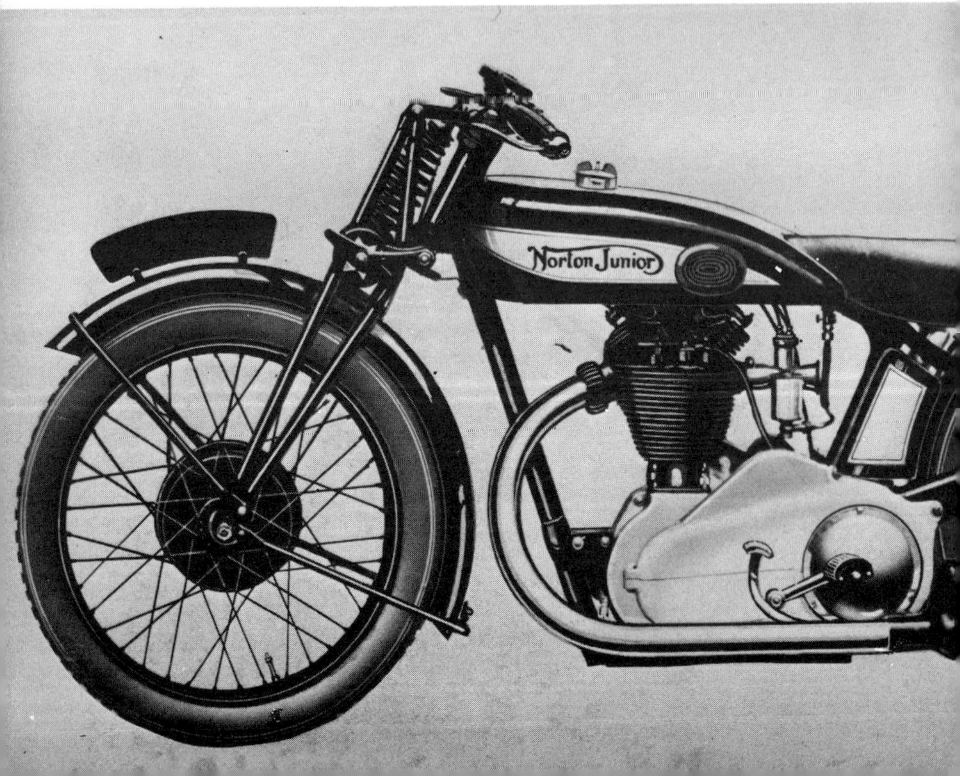
Norton Junior

Alec Bennett is congratulated on his 1927 Senior TT win on one of the first of the overhead camshaft Nortons

Prix and was placed second and third in the Grand Prix d'Europe and Ulster Grand Prix respectively.

What was the general appearance of the new camshaft model? Firstly the frame was of the more modern cradle pattern with both single top and front down tubes, in fact in the TT the push-rod motors were also fitted into the new frame. The fuel tank was of the complete 'saddle' type, dropping naturally over the top frame tube, but the exhaust pipe was still retained on the near side of the machine. Classification letters and numbers were given to both models with the pushrod version, soon to find favour with the sporting road rider, listed as the ES2, while the very new 'cammy' job would be known as the Model CS1.

Bert Denly, as busy as ever, made history by becoming the first rider of a 500cc machine (pushrod Norton) to cover one hundred miles in the hour in July 1927. Interesting also is the fact that other manufacturers reluctant to accept the superiority of the overhead camshaft design decided to stage a heavy attack in big time racing and famous marques such as Rudge, Whitworth and Sunbeam with their pushrod motors, reaping to some extent the development work pioneered by Nortons, carried all before them in the Isle of Man, at least until 1931, when the old form returned to Bracebridge Street racing machines.

Regardless of the fact that Norton fortunes were to decline in the road-racing world after 1927, due mostly to the intense concentration on development of the new overhead camshaft engines, the machines were still entered in the TT and other races, but alas with very disappointing results. To

After their success with the 500cc camshaft, Nortons included a 350cc model in their programme

date a Norton had won four TTs (excluding the pre-war twin-cylinder victory) with an overhead-valve motor of one kind or another, and eleven other classic road races. Such success was bound to advance a more ambitious programme and in 1928 Nortons extended their activities to include a team of Junior (350cc) models in the TT. A report appeared in *The Motor Cycle* in May where 'Ubique' writes: 'After much delay the long expected 350cc Norton has materialised, and its performance will be watched with the greatest interest. It is a typical "pushrod" Norton in every respect, and can hardly be distinguished from its larger brother except for its size and a modification to the rocker supports; the pivot bearings are lubricated from aluminium grease wells. The new Norton has received gruelling road tests in the hands of the men who will ride it in the great event, and has shown just those qualities which go to make a TT winner.' 'Ubique' refers to the new racing model as a typical 'push rod' Norton, for at the time he wrote his report, at least a month before the TT, two versions of this Junior machine had been produced, one in pushrod form and the other with the latest overhead camshaft design. It would appear that this journalist had only viewed the former model, for in the TT only the 'cammy' was raced. The power obtained from the 350 was naturally less than that of the 500s, the frames were therefore lightened by the modification of removing the middle pair of chain stays.

The Junior TT results were not very encouraging with all five official entries retiring, newcomer to the Team Jimmy Guthrie's machine catching fire, the ignition timing slipping on Stanley Wood's model, and of the remaining three, one being eliminated by a crash following some valve-spring trouble, another with a bent rocker, and the third suffering a broken valve. In the senior race Nortons faired a little better with fifth and sixth being the highest

placings. Despite the frustrating Isle of Man results however, later in the year Stanley Woods secured many firsts in continental races including a win in the 350cc class of the Dutch TT and a 500cc victory in the French Grand Prix.

In strict accordance with sales policy both the pushrod and camshaft machines were made available to the motorcycling public and were listed as Model 50 and Norton Junior, the Junior part being dropped early in 1929, and later all to be entirely superceded by the classifications CJ and JE respectively, the two models being in fact smaller editions of the already well proven CS1 and ES2 500cc mounts. Of the remaining motorcycles in the Norton range, the frames were very slightly redesigned in order to allow longer saddle tanks (now standard) to be fitted, the magnetos were however still positioned in front of the engine but now had shapely aluminium cases to protect them from the wet. Prices varied naturally according to each model with the CS1 500cc overhead camshaft machine being the most expensive at £90, while a model intended for sidecar work would sell at some twenty pounds less, but invariably both sidecar and motorcycle were sold as a complete unit making the total price about £95.10.0. In the hands of the sporting private owner the pushrod-operated overhead-valve Norton was still much a force to be reckoned with, but for prestige value the company would have to rely upon their works machines to forward the marque if sales were to continue successfully, thus for the 1929 season the pushrod engine was put aside and only the camshaft models were raced officially. In outward appearance the works models were not unlike those used in 1928, although the exhaust pipe had now been fitted on the off-side of the machine. Stanley Woods, Jimmie Simpson, and Jimmy Guthrie were numbers one, two and three in the team and were joined by the wealthy fun-loving Percy 'Tim' Hunt, a graduate from the Amateur TT ranks whose victories in 1927 and 1928 on Norton racers had impressed Walter Moore sufficiently to drag Tim from his bath a very short time following his second win.

It can be imagined just how exciting these years of the 'Twenties were, where any young man capable of proving himself in the racing game could be spotted by a works talent scout and thus to begin his professional road-racing career. Perhaps in all fairness a similar situation may exist today, but motorcycling was still a comparatively new sport, sales were booming and far less rigid controls tied the hands of anyone with initiative.

The TT Nortons, despite the very short trip into nostalgic thought, were still short of the necessary speed and reliability to win again the 'Blue Riband' of motorcycle racing. Of the four machines entered in the Junior race, all retired, three with valve-spring trouble and another with a faulty big-end bearing. The Senior event gave 'new boy' Hunt the opportunity to bring his machine home in fourth place behind a brace of Sunbeams and a Rudge, the other Nortons all having once again retired. It is worth mentioning details of Tim Hunt's Senior ride, for it must have been far from enjoyable. During the course of the race Hunt had fallen off twice, once at Quarter Bridge where one footrest was badly bent, and then on the mountain climb from Ramsey when the other footrest broke off completely. The situation demanded that virtually all the rider's weight was transferred to the

By 1929 racing Nortons started to possess the cobby look. The exhaust was now on the off-side of the machine. Jimmy Simpson is the rider

diminutive leather pad positioned on the rear mudguard, for the remainder of the race. Such enforced seating arrangements brought the suffering mudguard perilously near to the rear

The demoralising combination of Charlie Dobson and Sunbeam, who beat the two Nortons, not only here at Southport Sands but also in both the 1928 and 1929 Senior TTs. Number 5 is the famous Harry Langman

tyre in turn, and a bolt head on its underside ploughed a deep furrow around the tyre's tread. At this period Joe Craig had taken over as Norton's development engineer and it is known that he did not take kindly to anyone who dropped one of his precious models. However Tim must have surely vindicated himself by his spirited riding and it is hoped that in consequence he did not receive the usual 'blast'.

On production models new features

for 1929 were cast aluminium primary-chain cases on all pushrod and camshaft machines plus Webb forks of the central spring type. The side-valve range however retained the earlier pattern forks of Druid patent, not unsimilar to the Webb's but still possessing side-mounted springs.

If the TT results were a disappointment, the trials' world was doing very nicely with Norton machines gaining premier awards in the 'Colmore', 'Victory', 'Cotswold', 'Kickham', 'Travers', 'Alan', 'Southern', 'Scott', 'Bemrose' and 'West of England' Trials.

The shaky but interesting last years of the 'Twenties were passing away for Nortons. The 'Guvnor' had been dead for five years, but his tough, honest and undoubtedly masculine machines were well established on the markets of the world. The vintage years were gone, but there were signs that greater things were yet to come.

THE GOLDEN THIRTIES

The 1930 490cc 16H model, still with
left–hand exhaust pipe

The Vintage Motorcycle Club fixes the end of the vintage period at 31st December 1930, and its members' machines must have been manufactured not later than that date. There are some very slight exceptions to the rule however, for example modifications made by the manufacturer during 1930 which did not appear on catalogued machines until after the termination date. The cases are but few in number however and could not serve any real purpose in the preparation of this book. There are many respected members of the VMCC who will express in no uncertain terms their disapproval of most motorcycles produced between 1930 and 1939, and further maintain that such models contributed little, if anything, to the progress of the motorcycle industry at this time. Such has been the dislike of including 'youngsters' on the register, that a total disregard for the later machines is a well known, but tolerated fact. It was a pleasing moment for many dedicated enthusiasts however when a post-vintage class was introduced into

the club thus permitting, in the writer's view, some of the most glorious devices of the 'Thirties to participate in the various sporting events unique to this country.

To title this chapter the Golden Thirties should not be misunderstood, for those that suffered in the Depression of those years could justifiably ask what was golden about them, and this would be respected. The motorcycle industry bore its share of suffering and many fine companies simply went out of business overnight, at least in the early years of the decade. Where 1929 had been a boom year, a very opposite state of affairs now existed and motorcycles were indeed very hard to sell. Many well known London dealers for example were obliged to accept radio sets, bicycles, and in one or two cases even bedsteads on a part-exchange basis for any machine they wished to sell. Various concessions were made by the Chancellor of the Exchequer, Winston Churchill, to encourage the increased manufacture and subsequent sales and in his Budget Mr Churchill raised the weight limit for the £1.10.0 tax class of lightweight machines from 200 to 224 lbs and a number of manufacturers re-organised their designs and production in order to take full advantage of the concession. With a change of Government the whole thing was dashed. The road fund tax was roughly five per cent of the cost of the machine, and this was well to the fore in a prospective buyer's mind when choosing a machine. The industry protested but it was not until July 1930 that the 224 lb lightweight limit was finally conceded, thus leaving very little time to exhaust the 1930 models.

The Norton Company had never produced lightweight machines other than some rather rare devices in the very earliest years of the century, and regardless of the conditions of the time production of the normal range went ahead. The Norton had a name for utter reliability and would last its owner a lifetime if treated correctly, indeed it is to their credit that even some tragically neglected models are still giving the best of service to their pleasantly eccentric owners.

To cut the cost without paring the quality of the machine, lighting sets and pillion equipment were listed as extras, but for other than those incapable of improvising there was little worry and Norton sales went forward against the depressing tide.

It was evident that much thought and work had gone on behind the scenes at Bracebridge Street for both the standard range and the racing machines showed considerable changes. 1930 saw the introduction of cellulose paints and chromium plating, this last providing a very much harder and durable finish but in appearance not half so 'warm' as the nickel plate had been. Engine changes consisted of double-gear pump, dry sump lubrication, light alloy pistons, detachable cylinder-

The 588cc Model 19. A fine turn of speed and neater than ever

heads (where appropriate) and much shorter wheelbases. Formerly Pa Norton's slightly earlier models had been affectionately referred to as 'Ferrets' because their frames were long and low; now there existed a more cobby look about the machines, even so one felt one was sitting 'in' rather than 'on' the 1930 mounts, for the saddle position was still lower than the levels of the rear mudguard, petrol tank and steering head in turn.

A very important part of the Norton story was now to come, as far as the racing models were concerned, for in the next seven years with the Arthur Carroll redesigned overhead camshaft engine, remaining virtually unchanged in this period, the Nortons raced to victory after victory in a blaze of unapproachable glory.

Often described as the underrated genius of Norton Motors, Arthur Carroll had joined the Company in 1930 and proceeded to redesign the overhead camshaft engine. Carroll was to meet

his death in a motor accident five years later, but a fine tribute to his technical brilliance was surely shown by the fact that his new 'cammy' engines remained basically unchanged until 1937, two years after his death. The immortal Joe Craig was the development engineer, and the combination of Carroll's brain at the drawing board and Craig's great engineering ability in the development shop, plus (in its own way certainly as important) his great discipline, spelled success.

Walter Moore, originator of the first overhead camshaft engine at Bracebridge Street had left to take a post with the NSU concern in Germany. In consequence the racing models from the Neckarsulm factory bore a very strong resemblance in the 'Thirties to the Norton at least as far as the motor was concerned: but with a few exceptions the machines were far from competitive until the firm delved into the sphere of supercharging just before the Second World War.

The frames on the racing Nortons were very similar to those used in 1929, but the engines differed considerably; gone was the traditional 'blister', housing the bottom bevel gear on the off-side crankcase half, and in its place was the now familiar rectangular box. The crankcases were heavily ribbed on their exterior faces, and the mainshafts were of larger diameter, as also were the valves, their return springs being doubled in both cases. The rockers were fitted with needle roller bearings.

Where previously the engine possessed a tall and spindly appearance it now took on a more cobby look, no doubt contributed to by the addition of heavier finning on both barrel and cylinder head. Both Senior (500cc) and Junior (350cc) models had the relatively

Walter Moore's influence is evident on the 1930 500cc Super Sports NSU from Germany. During this period they were not really competitive on an international basis

new cradle frames, although the larger machine was provided with extra torque-stays to prevent whipping from the greater power that would be developed. Eight-inch diameter brakes were fitted to both wheels.

Already it was possible to purchase a standard road-going Norton with a four-speed gearbox, but the TT models retained the former pattern of three close ratios operated by the foot-change mechanism as in 1929. To complete the Norton inventory extra-large petrol tanks were fitted, and a gear-type oil pump. In order to ensure that an adequate supply of petrol-and-benzole mixture reached the carburettor, double float chambers were added.

It had been the custom to give the TT machines an airing by entering them for an Irish classic early in the season, the North West 200, held on the Port Stewart-Port Rush circuit. During the practice period the works Nortons had been screamed for mile after mile in first gear, as part of a special test, without blowing up. Some test. But for all that the TT results were again far from pleasing with the four-valve Rudges making it nearly a hat trick in both Senior and Junior races. To compensate for the beating in the Isle of Man, Stanley Woods, still the most successful member of the Norton team won several Grands Prix abroad. However the race enthusiast had not long to wait before he would see the Bracebridge Street 'ironware' dominate the Island.

How many really keen motorcycling types, lounging about the dispersal hut during the past war, eagerly awaited their turn to devour the pages of *Motor Cycling* and to read those famous articles by Graham Walker entitled 'Seen from the Saddle'? In one particular series Walker described in his usual brilliant journalistic style how the

The extrovert Percy 'Tim' Hunt with the Carroll-designed overhead camshaft engine in his works racer

Rudge marque lap by lap smashed the opposition in those 1930 TT events. In fact Nortons had really had their noses well and truly rubbed in the dust in the Junior race when the 350cc Rudge, straight from the drawing-board, punched home a one-two-three victory with its pushrod operated, overhead-(four) valve design, and four-speed gearboxes to boot. The latter point no doubt provided Joe Craig with food for thought where his future Nortons were to be considered. On the home front many modifications and additions were being made to the standard Nortons with detachable cylinder heads now available in the side-valve range. The new square oil tank and the petrol tank could be chromium plated for an extra twenty-five shillings on all-cradle frame and two-port models. The Model 20 made its appearance as an inexpensive, but of traditional high quality, 490-cc two (exhaust) port machine, and with a very much required item, a low lift spring-up stand. Handlebar instrument panels were also 'in' during 1930 and Nortons had produced a first-class design situated in the centre but just ahead of the handlebars, slightly tilted toward the rider for easy viewing.

Not listed in the range of Norton machines for 1930 was the Speedway model although several were in fact produced. Most of the current manufacturers had jumped on the band wagon when the newly introduced sport came to Great Britain during 1928, but in all fairness only the Douglas,

Rudge and to a certain degree Scott, in the correct hands, were game contenders for victory laurels. Norton could provide a suitable engine, but in the frame department much was left to be desired. It must be appreciated that dirt track racing as it was more often called demanded a very specialised type of machine, one that was totally unsuited for any form of road use (Douglas was an exception), a device that was required to be in   oadside for nine tenths of a race. The Norton took exception to this unfamiliar setting and was regarded as somewhat of a 'camel' to hold, and production ceased after a very short while, the factory being well able to employ their valuable time in producing models in their already well established range. Credit must go however to a then eighteen-year-old New Zealander Alf Mattson who won the Auckland Dirt Track Championships and numerous other events on a special machine. Mattson's frame was of his own construction, housing a specially tuned Norton ES2 engine. However New Zealand and Australian dirt tracks were much larger than our own, with definite straights of sometimes about half a mile and did not place such a premium on the frame parts. Bill Lacey, speedman extraordinary, won the Wakefield Cup Race at Brooklands on a specially bored-out Norton (586cc) at 108.27mph and in so doing became a Class D 750cc Champion for 1930. In the Swedish TT Gosta Anderson and

BUYER'S GUIDE FOR NORTON 1930

Model	Capacity	Valve System	Lubrication	Tyres	Weight	Price
J E	348cc	OHV	Dry Sump	26.3	305	£64 0 0
C J	348cc	OHC	Dry Sump	26.3	305	£72 0 0
16H	490cc	SV	Dry Sump	26.325	310	£49 10 0
18	490cc	OHV	Dry Sump	26.325	320	£59 10 0
20 (2 port)	490cc	OHV	Dry Sump	26.325	320	£64 15 0
E S 2	490cc	OHV	Dry Sump	26.325	325	£68 10 0
22 (2 port)	490cc	OHV	Dry Sump	26.325	325	£73 15 0
C S 1	490cc	OHC	Dry Sump	26.325	325	£79 10 0
19	588cc	OHV	Dry Sump	26.325	320	£62 0 0
Big Four	633cc	SV	Dry Sump	26.325	315	£54 0 0

All models have Sturmey three-speed gearboxes, with four speeds optional on some

Bertil Olsson were first and second on their overhead camshaft Nortons, while Stanley Woods on his 500 job won the important French Grand Prix at an average speed of 75.7mph. Harold Daniell, later to become one of the 'immortals' of Norton racing successes, had tasted the delights of high speed swervery in his first Manx Grand Prix (Amateur TT) on a 'same as you can buy' CS1 model.

On the mainland, small road-racing

Two-port 490cc Model 20, a style in line with other manufacturers

circuits such as Syston, situated between Grantham and Sleaford, were providing excellent racing 'for the lads', and at some of the early meetings Bill Rose and his Norton outfit could be relied upon to take care of the Sidecar classes, in no uncertain manner.

As the first year of the new decade drew to a close, 'Torrens' (Arthur B Bourne) was given the opportunity to ride Stanley Wood's racing Norton, the results of which formed the basis of an article about the man, Stanley Wood, and machine. It certainly made in-

teresting reading and one or two points are well worth repeating.

At Paddington Station the Norton was collected following its journey from Bracebridge Street, Birmingham, if anything looking perhaps a little strange as it was set up for road use and accordingly possessed acetylene lighting, bulb horn and standard silencer. In the article mention was made of Stanley's specially bent throttle lever, missing from the machine at this time, and causing 'Torrens' to remark that this was 'absolutely Stanley'. It would appear that like Alec Bennett during his Velocette days, Wood also had his own ideas on control of the carburettor slide, and contrary to the then more or less accepted practice of using twist grip control, he maintained a greater respect for the earlier lever system. Study of various photographs of the period show Wood's right hand not to be wrapped around the right handlebar end, rather is it in a sitting position upon the bar, with the thumb in close contact with the special lever. One imagines that Stanley, as clever as they could ever come, appreciated only too well how when one struck a bump at

Olympia 1931. The torpedo sidecar on the Norton stand is a great attraction

speed, the tendency was for the twist grip to shut off immediately, and additionally the lever system could provide some relief from the usual aching wrist experienced from the effort of holding open the twist grip against the force of a healthy slide spring, particularly when one was often in the racing saddle for more than two hours at a time.

Having perfected his own system, with the bend of the lever being 'just right', Norton's number one would remove the instrument after every race, it being replaced only when the Norton was to do battle again. 'Torrens' was thus obliged to use the lever from his own Norton, a 16H Model called 'Willing William'.

Wood's Norton was taken into the West Country and 'Torrens' was able to give readers of *The Motor Cycle* the 'feel' of this famous machine, describing everything as traditionally Norton with hairline steering, perfect road-holding, effortless power; indeed such were its excellent qualities that what appeared to be the start of an inevitable accident was averted, when approaching a trades van of some description. There is no doubt that Woods was a remarkably fit man, and the article contained details of the type of training he would do in preparation for a big race, with reference to having seen Wood in bathing trunks in the Isle of Man – 'A veritable Apollo with beautifully developed chest, calves and biceps'. Perhaps it would be fitting to conclude this chapter with a few brief words taken from the caption to a series of drawings in a 1930 copy of *The Motor Cycle. Competition Through The Artist's Eyes: Number 2. Racing.*

'The branch of the sport in which the foremost events, such as the TT races take place; a game that requires nerve, perfect physical fitness, brainwork, and an indomitable spirit in the man; and speed, stamina, and comfort in the machine.'

IN ASCENDANT

'The Manxman' pulls out into the
Mersey, bound for the Isle of Man
and the 1931 TT

Dennis May, one-time editorial staffman extraordinary of *Motor Cycling*, was held in the highest regard by all who found excitement in speed on two wheels. His very style transported a reader to a world of tyres, chains, heavy metal and the quite undescribable smell of burnt Castrol 'R'; the very ingredients of motorcycle racing. In a series of profiles published some years ago May covered the racing careers of several stars of the Golden Era, of which Norton riders Tim Hunt and Stanley Woods were a certainty for inclusion. Came 1931, and Nortons were to embark on their fantastic run of successes, indeed perhaps their greatest years. No apologies are made for presenting Dennis May's words as he wrote them in his description of Stanley Wood's and Tim Hunt's ride in the German Grand Prix; the atmosphere of Nortons in Anger forty years ago.

'That awe inspiring congolmeration of convolutions and switchbacks in the Eifel Mountains, the setting for the 1931 German Grand Prix. The issue, it was obvious, would lie between Tim Hunt and Stanley Woods, and before the start it was decreed by Mr Bill Mansell, then Norton's Boss, that the pair should preserve peace until the start of the last lap, then race to win. They duly conformed to this order of the day, virtually turning nine-tenths of the Prix into an extended rolling start. But finally at the drop of the invisible hat, the fur really flew. Hunt, who says "I always liked corners" decided in advance where "deo volente" he would drop it across the Dubliner, who expectedly went into a short lead at the start of the last lap. The Hunt plan was to get Woods on the outside of a very fast turn close to the finish. But the Nurburgring is over fourteen miles round, and several things happened before that hairy big climax. Topping one of the circuit's notorious blind brows Tim fluffed a gear change and went from third into second instead of into top, and in consequence nearly spilling him over the front number plate. Then at the celebrated Karussel Turn,

which is the nearest approach to a Wall of Death that is to be found in this road racing world, Woods made a superhuman effort to rid his slipstream of Hunt, and in the process came within an inch of going over the abrupt lip of the wall. When in due course the duellists roared down to the corner that Tim had earmarked for the showdown, Woods, a superior mind-reader, delayed his braking to the last split-second, obviously intent on taking the turn at a speed that would make passing impossible. But Hunt, knowing it was now or never, veered out to a line that even for him was crazily wide, and deferred his cut-off later still. Both his wheels overran the road verge, throwing up a miniature wave of loose sand. Hunt's Norton slid broadside for fifty yards, but when he finally got the thing on an even keel, he was leading the race by half a length. One more hazard to go, this was a flat out S bend. Into it the pair plunged, Stanley's front wheel almost nuzzling Tim's rear. When they came out and headed for the home stretch of concrete the two Nortons were dead abreast. Inch by inch in a last Homeric spurt, Woods gained. With both riders' chins practically denting their tank tops, they gunned over the line. The Irishman was first by half a wheel.

Such dramatic scenes were to be re-enacted time and time again by the victorious Norton Teamsters, indeed such was their more or less 'guaranteed' success, that one may be forgiven for describing their brilliant efforts as being of monotonous regularity, so much so that coverage of the seven years until 1937 has provided some headache in an attempt to prevent the narrative becoming somewhat tedious. For fear of the inevitable repetition, the years in question are presented in tabulated form, seasoned from time to time with interesting items appropriate to a particular year.

Nineteen thirty-one. Inlet ports reshaped on racing Nortons to accept down draught carburettors. 18mm plugs discarded in favour of 14mm.

Fitting of semi-slipper type pistons, to prevent the possibility of both cracking and seizures. New engine shaft shock-absorber of the rubber buffer type. Four speed gearboxes (Sturmey) operated by the positive foot-change mechanism, the old kick-change system having been discarded some three years earlier. Cast aluminium centre stands, the old rear stands being too heavy, but nevertheless used in practice periods, prior to a big race. New shock absorber, mounted on lower fork link assembly, operated by a large handwheel, with instant adjustment from the saddle. Snap-on filler caps.

Tim Hunt wins both classes of TT try out, the North West 200 in Ireland and is tipped to bring off the double in the Isle of Man. Some minutes after winning the Junior TT event, Hunt, between gulps of stone ginger, firstly praised the excellent handling of his Norton and said the 'engine was lovely'. The bumpy bit before Kirk-michael he did not enjoy at all, but

Bill Lacey's record breaking Norton, beautifully prepared as always, and with a track-type gear change system

beyond the detachment of his plug terminal on the first lap he had no untoward incidents to report. Jimmy Guthrie, the second man home, was as quiet and reticent as usual and mentioned that he did not have much time to fall off. Full of praise for his Norton he had jokingly remarked that his only complaint was that the engine 'could not do 200' because he felt that with the weather and the course as they were, he could have got around quite comfortably. He reported a slight headache as a result of 'lying down to it', but that was all.

It should have been a one-two-three victory for Nortons, for the other Jimmy (Simpson), a potential winner always, had the race in his pocket. It was cruel luck therefore that he was 'outed' temporarily by a trivial stop. Just before the Bungalow section his engine was loth to do more than a crawl. Thinking it might have been a plug, he fitted a new one, to no avail however, and he therefore decided to retire. He accepted a drink, no doubt from a sympathetic spectator, lit a cigarette, signed some autograph books, and then suddenly had a brainwave. He took out the main jet and found it

almost sealed with dirt. He cleared it, and all lost horses returned. A quicker diagnosis could not have saved him the race, but it might have given him second place. Simpson eventually finished eighth, while Stanley Woods crossed the line in fourth place, beaten by that veritable little ball of dynamite Ernie Nott on his works Rudge.

The Senior results were even better with Hunt, as forecast, winning from Guthrie and Woods respectively. Stanley's ride was not without incident, rather minor, but annoying things happened such as the petrol filler cap that would just not close, requiring a glove to be stuffed in the hole in consequence.

Jimmy Simpson made fastest lap at over eighty miles an hour, the first occasion on which the Island Course had been lapped at such a speed, but alas retired during the race.

Norton Team won ten Grands Prix and were placed third in four of them. Norton standard range of models virtually unchanged from 1930. His Majesty The King of the Belgians placed another order for a British motorcycle. King Albert was then over fifty years of age, was a keen sportsman, and took an interest in moun-

taineering and aviation as well as motorcycling. His new mount was a Norton, the third machine of the make that he had owned. The King was a tall man and had the brake position altered to suit him, and had also expressed a wish to have the rear chain totally enclosed.

Nineteen thirty-two. Those two well seasoned racing men Alec Bennett and Freddie Dixon were talking freely to the Press about the demise of the single-cylinder racing engine and the need for multi-cylinder units to replace it as soon as possible. Norton in concert with other manufacturers stated that it might be desirable, but the cost would be terrific, and while they were winning so many races with comparative ease using the proven single-cylinder engines, they were not immediately concerned. It was stated that HRH Prince George was to visit the Isle of Man to watch the Senior TT in June. Prince George and his brothers had in the past taken a keen interest in the

Kim Collett and passenger 'all out' at Donington Park, 1932: an early appearance of the Special 596cc Norton engine

sport and the Duke of York (later King George VI) besides being a keen motorcyclist himself, entered a machine and rider for a number of Brooklands events.

Bill Lacey had covered 110.8 miles in one hour at Montlhery, on a Norton. The Inter-Varsity speed trials at Hexton Manor, near Luton, the home of Sir James Hill Bart. A description of the scene on that mid-February day is most pleasing. 'Enthusiasts worked away at an assortment of motorcycles, wearing in most cases that utterly roguish look that comes of removing the fuel tank, and substituting something about the size of a cocoa tin. Their friends wandered around asking where numbers could be obtained. Fierce looking gentlemen in white overalls played devastating arpeggios on Bugatti

A classic racing Norton to the last nut and bolt. This model provided Stanley Woods with his second Senior TT victory for Bracebridge Street in 1932

throttle pedals. Officials played with miles of telephone wire apparently not in the least bit worried by the fact that it was one half hour past the advertised starting time.' Malcolm Muir (Cambridge University) won the 350cc event on a Velocette, and made two third best times in the 500cc and unlimited capacity classes on his Norton. 'Spug' Muir had already won the 1931 Senior Manx Grand Prix, and later in 1932 was to win the classic Hutchinson '100' at Brooklands.

Syston and Donington Park Road races, Easter Monday, 1932. Appropriately called the Dolphin Cup Race, held in a shower of rain, the irresistible George Richards (Scott in sidecar) was freely tipped as the winner provided his motor could stand the towsing. However those in the know (a delightful expression) said 'watch George ''Kim'' Collett' for although he was down in the programme to ride a 588cc Norton and sidecar he was to actually use a very special 596cc overhead camshaft engined outfit. A terrific

battle took place between Richards and Collett until Collett's magneto worked loose, and he retired from the contest. Richards won, with C E Williams (490 Norton s/c) second, while Bill Rose, also Norton mounted was third. More will be written about the type of Norton engine that Kim Collett was using, for it formed the basis of the power units that most of Britain's greatest sidecar aces were to employ in the immediate pre- and post-Second World War, National and World Championship meetings.

Over at Donington, Jimmy Simpson made a very unusual appearance but was not placed in his events, although Dennis Mansell, son of the then Norton managing director Bill Mansell, won the sidecar race on his 490cc outfit, while C D Bruce was third on a 495cc model, the capacity suggesting rather a special motor. Imports of motorcycles into New Zealand revealed that out of 1,601 registrations fifty-six were Norton.

Stanley Woods took third place in the

Senior race of the North West 200. TT Nortons were very little different from the previous year, other than more generous finning of the cylinder barrel and head, Senior models had a compression ratio of 7.25 to 1, while the weight of the complete machine was 312 lbs. Tyre sizes for both 500cc and 350cc models were 21 inches by $3\frac{1}{2}$ inches rear, and 21 inches by 3 inches front. The Junior machines had compression ratios of 7.5 to 1, while in turn their weight was 298 lbs. Certain weight saving measures were taken by the fitting of dural mudguards and special alloys for clutch and front brake levers. An extraordinary long front brake lever was used and gave the rider considerably more power over control. Wheel rims were made of a special light gauge steel, these weight paring matters applying to both Senior and Junior models. Larger petrol and oil tanks allowed three and a half gallons of fuel and three quarters of a gallon of oil to be carried. The very comfortable Dunlop little rubber racing saddle, that permitted a rider to actually walk away from his machine after some 265 road racing miles.

At the Whitsun meeting at Syston, Harold Daniell enjoyed a field day on his CS1 Norton, including the Manx Race, the prize being the necessary expenses to help a rider to enter for the September races in the Isle of Man. Harold was a really tough character, and, in the way of the racing man of the early 'Thirties, would load up his Norton sidecar float with the CS1, prop his brother on the pillion, and with tins of dope, tools, chains, leathers and every other piece of paraphernalia required by the racing man, set out from his Forest Hill home, win races at Syston on one day of the Public Holiday, cross over to Donington, putting up at the famous Hall over night; and then proceed to clean up most classes on the famous Leicestershire Circuit. In discussion with Harold some years ago, he said that both he and his brother were just about fagged after two days of racing, plus the various journeys involved, but with 'some tidy wins beneath one's belt we found heart to sing as we thumped the old Norton float back to London'.

Norton TT racers carried experimental tension springs, mounted on the forks to act as dampers.

The official Norton team for the TT Tim Hunt and Stanley Woods plus the Jimmys Simpson and Guthrie. Three additions were the New Zealand rider Mattson (of Auckland Speedway fame) plus the original 'Muscle Man' S 'Ginger' Wood, and C B Taylor. Both Wood and Taylor retired in the Junior race, while there was no further mention of Mattson at all, presumably he was a non-starter. Stanley Woods won the Junior and Senior races; in the latter event Guthrie and Simpson were second and third. The Groote Prijs van Nederland – The Dutch TT Senior class won by Tim Hunt with Stanley Woods second. Reverse finishing order in the 350cc race.

The French Grand Prix with Woods and Hunt first and second in the 500cc class. Jimmy Simpson won the Junior event, admittedly the French Jonghi opposition did not materialise as all three works machines packed up in

Hero worship for Freddie Frith, fifth home in the Senior Grand Prix in the September of Woods's TT victory year

the early stages of the race, but this was no lesser credit to Jimmy who always appreciated a fight, in the most sporting sense of the word. Charlie Dodson was considered to be the menace at the Belgian Grand Prix at Francorchamps. Charlie was riding an extremely fast Excelsior JAP and the Norton camp eyed him with every caution. During the course of the 500cc race Dodson struck a terrific bump when very well placed, the impact being such that he suffered a dislocated shoulder, and was taken in great pain to a local doctor who soon put matters right with Charlie out to the world 'under a whiff of gas'. Tim Hunt was also a casualty when he broke his collarbone. The results were: Senior race; Woods first at 77.66mph while Simpson and Guthrie were first and second in the Junior event at 72.94 and 72.93mph respectively – a very close race indeed. At St Andrews during July 1932 Jimmy 'G' riding his 490cc Norton for the Hawick Club won the twenty mile 600cc sand racing championship, and also the unlimited class.

Donington Park, August Monday. The great 'Character' George Vesey, a Nottingham Clubman, put it across the 'regulars' on their sophisticated camshaft Nortons, riding his famous Norton 'flat tanker' of earlier vintage. Stanley Woods won both classes of the Swiss

Grand Prix. In the Ulster Grand Prix, at one time the world's fastest road race, Woods won the 500cc event at 85.15mph while Tim Hunt, now back in action, was second at 84.18mph.

An interesting article appeared in the pages of *The Motor Cycle* in which 'Torrens' described the camshaft International Norton as the ideal model for high speed touring and in so doing caused many a frustrated speed enthusiast to rush to the shed to plant a well aimed kick at his modest touring side valve.

In the Manx Grand Prix in September Norman Gledhill and Harold Daniell took first and second places on their Nortons in the Senior race. Meanwhile a young man by the name of Frith motored home in fifth place in that event on a 350 Norton.

During the autumn of 1932 the Norton factory introduced two additions to their already generous list of road models, for release in 1933. There were to be single- and twin-port editions of a new 350cc model, catalogued as the 50 and 55. The two machines, apart from differing exhaust systems, were identical, with 71mm bore and 88mm stroke. The object in the mind of the manufacturers was to offer to the public a 350cc machine of high performance at a price rather below that which was possible with the overhead camshaft design. In line with

the current Norton practice, a gear-type oil-pump attended to the dry sump lubrication system, while the magneto was chain-driven from the camshaft, and positioned behind the cylinder. A pressed steel cover protected the primary chain and a system of automatic lubrication was arranged from the crankcase breather, thus a fairly steady oil mist was sprayed onto the primary drive. A four-speed gearbox was fitted as standard and gear selection was either by hand or foot according to the customer's wishes, although an extra charge was made if the foot system was required. Tyre sizes were 19 inches by 3.25 inches on the special Norton quickly detachable and interchangeable wheels, while the brakes were of seven-inch diameter. Both standard and the more sporting upswept pipes could be supplied, and it was claimed that a speed of seventy miles per hour was well within the capabilities of either model.

A new silencer of the venturi pattern also made its debut at this time, not unlike the famous 'Brookland's Can' in appearance. Inside the silencer body was a pepper-pot baffle that silenced the exhausting without impairing the efficiency of the engine, and the whole assembly was set off with a pleasing

The single-port version Model 50 of 350cc

fishtail end. Unlike many silencers of the period, this device could be readily dismantled for cleaning purposes.

All petrol and oil tanks were now chromium plated, with aluminium enamelled centre panels, and as an addition a very neat instrument panel could be supplied to fit into a suitable recess in the tank top The panel also incorporated a rain gutter which prevented the rain from driving hard down onto a rider's crutch during bad weather. The design was ingenious for the complete instrument assembly could be removed, when the complete fuel-tank in turn was to be taken off, without detaching or indeed disturbing any of the electrical wiring. The hub caps on all models were plated which gave the wheels a distinctive appearance. Only the side-valve range retained three-speed gearboxes, while all pushrod over-head-valve models had improved rocker ends which in turn made line contact on the valve stem end.

Montlhéry, 1932. Norton rider Debay, winner of the 500cc race, in discussion with Prince Nicholas of Roumania

A notable change was made on the Model 19, which was now of increased capacity. The pushrod overhead-valve system was retained, as was the main features of the cycle parts, but the bore and stroke had been changed to 82mm by 113mm giving a capacity of 596cc, eight cubic centimetres more. The thinking behind this move was to provide a dual purpose machine, suited for fast solo or sidecar work. For the speedman modifications were made to the International Models, for true to their policy of producing real TT replicas, the makers incorporated the 1932 cylinder-head on these machines. Larger caged roller bearings were employed in the rocker pivots and the rockers themselves were of more sturdy construction. In addition oil leads were taken to each valve guide direct from the rocker box, and eventually this modification was extended to all overhead camshaft engines. The TT forks with the hand-controlled friction damper were now standardised. Other refinements on the 'Inters' were chromium plated wheel rims, spokes and brake drums, and improved metal tool boxes.

To wind up the year 1932, Debay won the Montlhéry Grand Prix on his Norton with Prince Nicholas of Rumania in attendance as interested spectator. Stanley Woods passed on his tip for clearing rain-spattered goggles; by the simple expedient of sewing a piece of chamois leather to the back of his racing glove, and a crafty wipe from time to time.

The old argument of 'Have we reached the limit in racing speeds?' appeared for the umpteenth time in the correspondence columns of the motor-cycling press. The top speed of a genuine works racing Norton (500cc) being incidentally about 108 to 111mph at this period. In the early months of 1933 the South Reading Club's 'Three Musketeers Trial' was held, the Sidecar Cup winner being H R Taylor (490cc Norton s/c) and the 350cc Solo Cup to B L Matterson; the two names will be familiar to many as partners in the famous South London Norton Agency.

April and preparations were under way for the North West 200. Norton racing machines changed very little from 1932: wheel rims were slightly narrower, while the width of the front

THE 1933 NORTON RANGE

International Model 30	490cc	OHC	£90 0 0
International Model 40	348cc	OHC	£82 10 0
Model 50 single port	348cc	OHV	£53 0 0
Model 55 twin port	348cc	OHV	£55 0 0
Model 16H	490cc	SV	£49 15 0
Model Big Four	633cc	SV	£54 0 0
Model 18 single port	490cc	OHV	£59 0 0
Model 20 twin port	490cc	OHV	£62 0 0
Model 19 single port	596cc	OHV	£62 0 0
Model ES2 single port (cradle frame)	490cc	OHV	£62 10 0
Model CJ	348cc	OHC	£67 10 0
Model CS1	490cc	OHC	£75 0 0

NORTON SIDECARS

Special Sports Model K	£18 10 0
Sports Touring Model L	£19 5 0
Full Touring Model M	£22 10 0

All available to suit Norton machines and these were fitted with detachable wheels and interchangeable with those of the motorcycle

brakes was appreciably increased. Formerly extra long brake and clutch levers were made of aluminium, now steel pressings.

New steering damper made its appearance and turned out to be unusually neat in construction. A central bolt served the dual purpose of holding the damper assembly in the steering-head by means of a cone expanding a sleeve and of holding the top-cap by means of which the friction plates were tightened down against each other. These plates presented a much larger surface than usual and the body of the damper was so formed as to render the assembly waterproof.

The cylinder-heads were made of a special alloy, in fact a bronze skull,

around which was cast an aluminium-silicon alloy shell. The cylinder barrels were also of bi-metal construction in which aluminium fins were cast on to a cast-iron liner. Drip-feed system attached to the oil tank took care of primary chain lubrication. Stanley Woods won the North West 200 in the 500cc class at 73.62mph. Tim Hunt came first in the 350cc class at 71.40mph. 'Woods wins by five seconds' read the headlines in *The Motor Cycle* following Stanley's Junior TT victory. Tim Hunt and Jimmy Guthrie, second and third in turn.

Woods finished in his usual fresh and cheerful condition. He reported that he had had a very satisfactory ride, though he admitted having had one or two hectic moments. Apparently at some points around the course sand had been put down to counteract any stickiness that might have developed in the tar. He

Norton 'Golden Boys' in 1933. Woods leads Hunt at the Virage de la Maison Blanche, Dieppe Grand Prix

made this discovery in the Governor's Bridge dip on the first time round and thereafter looked out for it. Later he encountered what appeared to be a fresh supply put down at Ramsey Hairpin just on his usual riding line, and it caused him an anxious moment. On his last lap, just above the Gooseneck he ran onto the grass: 'Looking at the flappers' instead of at the road was his excuse.

Tim Hunt was not terribly informative, but reported that he had an absolutely trouble-free run, his only worry having been the myriads of Manx flies. To add a little sauce to the results of the Norton victory, Jimmy Guthrie had several adventures to report. On the first lap he hit the bank at Hillberry and found to his surprise and relief that a bent footrest was the total extent of the damage. He was able to forget this mishap in the course of his

long scrap with Jimmy Simpson later to retire, which lasted for three laps. On the fifth lap he was unlucky again, falling at Quarter Bridge. His machine escaped this time with bent handlebars and footrests (This would have certainly pleased Joe Craig no end), while he got off with a scraped arm and fingers. Regardless of these troubles Jimmy must have ridden a very spirited race for he finished only two miles an hour slower than Hunt.

With Simpson's retirement, Nortons could not bag the Team Prize (a consolation for the well-ridden Velocettes). Some idea of the perfect preparation of the Nortons may be gained from the fact that when all three motors were stripped, they looked internally as though they had been for little more than a gentle 200-mile tour, truly remarkable, for the punishment a racing motorcycle received on the

Jack Williams, most successful of the Norton Trials riders, with his overhead camshaft engined model. Note the attempts to waterproof certain vital parts of the machine

island course was beyond description.

Practice brevities prior to the Senior TT.

Douglas, Tuesday June 6th 1933.

This morning Simpson, Guthrie and Woods were the first to take it more or less 'flat' and they came by in a solid ear-splitting phalanx.

Douglas, Wednesday 7th June.

Stanley Woods has been the first to do it on his third circuit this morning and he had intended to do four, doubtless for a consumption test; he smashed the race lap record with a perfectly lunatic average of 81.9mph. From what one could gather from various points, and from personal inspection at Hillberry he took no chances, except perhaps that he occasionally braked to the limit before entering bends.

Douglas, Friday 9th June.

At the foot of Bray Hill this morning the usual little crowd received the usual big thrills in exchange for the severe discomforts of leaping out of bed (figuratively speaking) at 4 o'clock in the morning. The bend and bumps at the foot certainly show up road worthiness and the Nortons ·must be given this morning's prize. Simpson, Guthrie and Hunt came down together on full bore with their front wheels pawing the air, yet all three were as steady as if they had been miraculously locked together.

Woods, Simpson and Hunt came first,

second and third, Jimmy Guthrie fourth. Seven Nortons started in the race with Jack Williams, the well known trials rider, in tenth place while J H Pringle, the Commonwealth representative, finished in twentieth position, and there was one retirement.

The Dutch TT, the Swiss Grand Prix, the French and the Belgian all won by Norton. For the German Grand Prix, the Nortons had not been entered, a disappointment for the German BMW riders who had been very eager to do battle with the Birmingham brigade. The reasons behind the non-entry are interesting: The usual home of the 'German' had been the famous Nurburgring, but a decision had been made in 1933 to transfer to the ultra-fast Avus Track near Berlin, a fantastic place if ever there was, with two very long straights linked by banked curves at either end. The BMWs entered for the Senior event were in pukka track trim running on dope fuel, and their handlebar ends terminating not far short of front wheel spindle height. The Norton works were not prepared to play this particular game although it certainly would have been quite a spectacle as riders of the Woods, Simpson, Guthrie and Hunt ilk fought it out with the German 'cracks'. For the Ulster Grand Prix, blond bombshell Walter Rusk from Ireland joined the Norton Team, and rode into second place behind Woods in the Senior race. Norton policy being no doubt 'We cannot be better served than by a "local" who knows his native roads like the back of his hand'.

The Swedish Grand Prix, and injuries suffered by Tim Hunt during the 500cc race were to put paid to his brilliant career of motorcycle racing. Already Stanley Woods had suffered the wild caprices of a rebellious engine in the senior race. Perhaps the Nortons, so finely tuned to accept a petrol/benzole mixture as their only acceptable brew, took exception to the changes that the Swedish organisers had permitted in the usage of alcohol. Before the troubles however both Woods and

'Blond bombshell' Walter Rusk, Norton team member of the early 1930s

Hunt were performing to perfection their invisible towrope act until the 'thirteenth' lap when Hunt, who was tailing Woods into a very fast bend came upon the 250cc rider Lundberg (FN) who having experienced some trouble with his motor looked down in an attempt to make some adjustment to the carburettor. Such action even at modest speeds may cause a wobble, which was precisely what happened to Lundberg. It was impossible for Hunt to miss him and the two collided very heavily. The FN rider was killed instantly while the Norton ploughed into a tree, resulting in a broken thigh and severe arm injuries for Hunt. Treatment lasted many months, indeed he was to lie on his back for nine of them, and for five years he was obliged to use crutches. Sadly, Tim's racing days were now over.

During the tragic collision, by sheer masterly riding, Woods had avoided being involved in the melee, although he was to retire on his nineteenth lap. For once the famous Norton Team were not to stand on the winner's rostrum to receive their laurels. At Bilbao in Spain, Jimmy Guthrie won both Junior and Senior classes of the Spanish TT while at home the Streatham and District MCC organised revival of path racing at Crystal Palace, with local lad Harold Daniell winning most classes on his cammy Norton, compulsory Brooklands silencer and all.

Show time at Olympia: Worth seeing there, famous racing riders probably in bowler hats. Alas nowadays such a piece of classic headgear would be worn in a way best described as 'with vulgar gimmick'.

Certain very slight additions were made to the standard Nortons for the 1934 programme, to provide the rider with even greater pleasure in his motorcycling. Most noticeable was the new oil-bath chaincase for the primary drive, fitted even to the International models, although here there was the alternative of a light guard if so required. Obviously with an oil-bath chaincase the clutch had to be impervious to oil, and Nortons had designed their own special clutch using special Ferodo fabric inserts in turn, and after many tests the clutch, also fitted with a shock absorber, was pronounced fit for service.

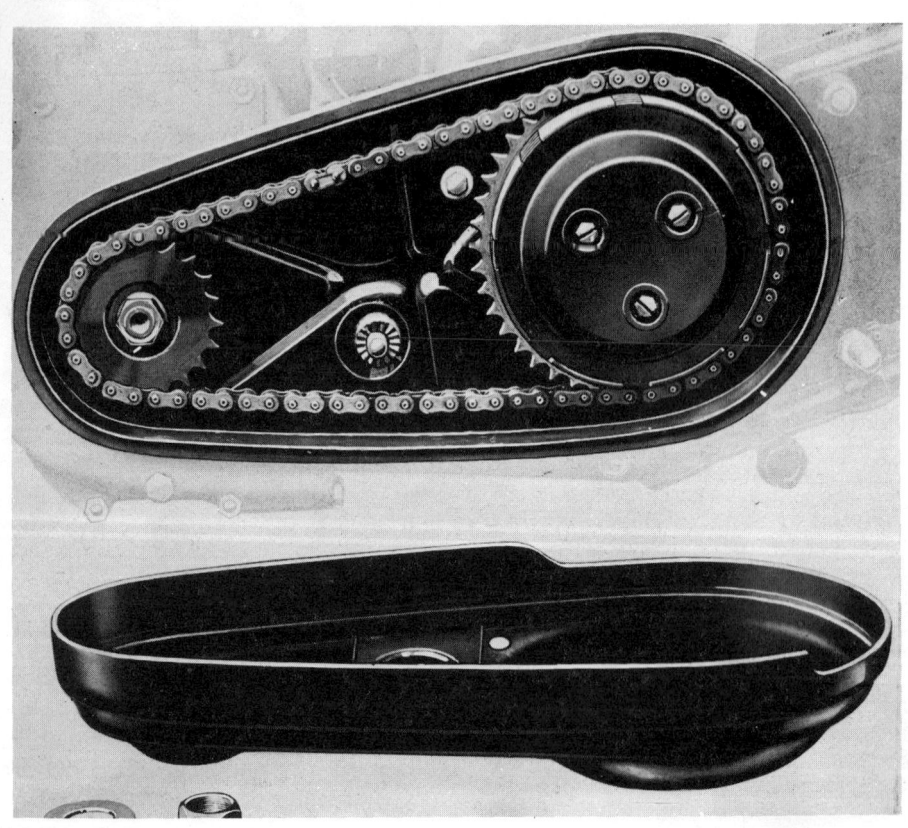

The famous racing forks with their additional check springs were incorporated on all models, and four-speed gearboxes were made standard throughout the range, although the choice of hand or foot control still remained, with an extra charge for the TT-type positive foot change mechanism.

Another rather novel idea was a small sump for trapping impurities, provided below the scavenger intake pipe, and in the case of the International models a second sludge-trap was placed below the filter in the lower bevel box. On all overhead-valve models there was a direct feed from the rocker box to each valve guide.

As a direct result of racing experience, narrower front hubs were fitted to the 'Inters'. The hub shells, brake drums, and spoke flanges were in a single piece, allowing also for

Above: Check springs on the forks, soon to become a famous Norton feature. Left: A new innovation, the oil-bath primary chain case assembly

narrower forks in which the weight-saving was considerable. Other details in the process of cleaning up were a modified handlebar shape, a quicker and smoother twist grip action, some silencer improvements and the Lucas rubber-mounted battery.

The CS1 and CJ camshaft models, in many ways similar to the Internationals, had cradle frames, a slightly higher ground clearance and smaller tanks. And that was that for the plus-foured, leather-coated enthusiast of 1933.

Nineteen thirty-four. A peep behind the scenes at Bracebridge Street racing development shop with our dear friend 'Torrens', a lengthy interview with Joe Craig. Craig proceeded as follows: 'No serious experiments can be carried out during the racing season because of lack of time. Even between the last of the big Continental events and the Ulster Grand Prix there are only weeks. Each racing season provides its lessons. New ideas will have occurred. Hardly is the year's racing at an end than work starts upon the machines to be used the following season. Over the winter months these fresh ideas have to be tried out, and all the lessons put to good use. There is always plenty to do.'

The various ideas are worked out in collaboration with Arthur Carroll of the drawing office, Carroll is Craig's right hand man and a brilliant ever ready help. Making the 'bits' may sound a very short job but possibly the particular bit involves a new casting; after the design has been thought out there will be drawings to make, then a special pattern to be fashioned out of wood, next the foundry work which, as the casting is not a production job, is almost sure to take time, and finally there is the machining and building up. Even the smallest changes take time, and time says Joe Craig is the biggest factor that has to be contended with in developing a TT engine.

Joe works entirely on test bench results. The road generally is the form of the first races of the year and is only used to check the results of the Heenan and Froude water-brake. The engines only are tested.

'What about the frames?', asked 'Torrens'. Craig replied: 'Except for a certain amount of lightening, the well known cradle frame has been the same for '31, '32, '33, and now for '34'. The winter is devoted entirely to the design and manufacture of the parts and testing and developing engines.

When questioned on how long it takes to build TT engines, Craig replied that it was impossible to say, but given the parts as they left the tool room the fitter would put them together in a matter of six hours. This though an art in itself was only assembly, there was all that work that goes before it, that turning which means that every part is perfectly made, is in perfect alignment, and all are fitted together to form, as nearly as human skill can ensure, a perfect whole. There are no secrets of tune said Craig, not one. It is design plus workmanship plus fitting. At one time there were secrets, such as moving the contact breaker round in relation to the armature spindle so that the best possible spark was obtained at high engines speeds, but that was in the days before they knew everything about magnotos. All that had changed now.

'Torrens' then turned to the question of actual work carried out on the bench. Each alteration is tried out by itself. One thing at a time is the inviolable rule, because then and then only is it possible to say whether the modification is an advantage or not. Perhaps the change is in regard to the shape of an inlet port. This port only will be modified and the results obtained checked off against previous results. A log of everything is kept, so in the course of time there is an enormous store of definite data to draw upon.

Joe showed one of his log books.

As you will notice this relates to a special test on an engine for the last Ulster Grand Prix carried out in order to compare two different exhaust arrangements. The row of figures on the right is those obtained with one of these

ULSTER 350cc No 6

August 3rd 1934 Bar 29.4 ins Temp 72°F	Long TT exhaust pipe	490 short pipe. Short flare 4 ins
4,000rpm	19¾	20
4,500rpm	20 −	20½ −
5,000rpm	20	20¼ +
5,500rpm	19¾ +	20¼ −
6,000rpm	18¾ +	19¼/19½
6,500rpm	17	17½

exhaust trumpets, familiarly known as 'loud speakers'. At the top are notes of atmospheric pressure and temperature, and on the extreme left the revolutions per minute, while the other two rows of figures show the actual readings on the brake. The comparison between the two sets of results is interesting.

On the question of compression ratios, Craig advised that he would insist upon the highest one that could be usefully employed, a first class rider, he added, will use successfully the highest ratio that an engine, as proved by bench tests, can stand with advantage. Such a ratio means that there will be detonation at low engine speeds, but in any case speeds below 3,500rpm are no use from the point of view of engine performance. Even above this speed there will be slight detonation if the highest useful compression ratio be employed, but not so much as to affect power output.

'Torrens' then passed onto other items that must receive some form of bench testing to which Craig replied: 'We must test valve-springs for reliability, they must be strong enough to prevent bounce yet no stronger': Could he detect loss of power with strong springs? 'No, the chief reason why they must not be too strong is for the simple reason that they will spell increased wear on the valve gear.

Sparking plugs must undergo their own test, for if a plug is too hot there is a chance that it will oil up as a machine dives into a bend. In the TT there is of course always the question of riders having to get off the mark with .cold engines. (Craig was speaking to Arthur Bourne of course in 1934 – a warming-up period for TT machines was introduced the following year).

On the other hand, Craig continued, the plug must be able to stand up to the compression ratio and to the petrol/benzole, not the kindest of fuels from the plug's point of view.

'Torrens' further questioned: 'When testing an engine for reliability, how many hours do you give it?' Craig replied: 'A very long test is one of three and one half hours at peak revs and full load. If nothing happens in that time there is no point in carrying on because this is as long as the race will be and far more drastic because there is no shutting off, as for instance at corners'.

This gives an inkling as to the months and months of work that goes on behind the scenes. By the time the North West 200 or Leinster 200, whichever is first, comes along, the machines are built and ready. These, the first big races of the year, form the real preliminary test, they afford the try-out prior to the Isle of Man and the annual tour of the Continent. Here is where the riders praise or condemn the man responsible for all that work put in during the winter. The machines themselves by the way are almost as alike as two peas, usually the only difference between a brace of 500s is in the footrests which are designed to suit the individual rider. Generally the pukka TT jobs appear in the two races mentioned. On their return after the first race the machines are stripped and examined. The main things learned are really in the nature of checks. There are two important questions to be answered, whether the modifications made over the winter have altered the top gear ratio, and the compression ratio that the engines will stand. It is the unexpected that happens, if you will excuse this trite old phrase – and this is what the man responsible has to guard against in preparing the machines for a race.

You will not find the racing Nortons swathed in 'Insulating tape' (the motorcyclist's usual term). Indeed Craig would look upon its need as an insult to his workmanship. He maintains that a nut will not work loose if its face is true with the threads, and the internal threads and those on the bolt are properly cut. There is however one place that you will find tape and that is largely a matter of bowing to convention – the caps on the tyre valves are taped. As for the driving chains, the primary is always endless, while the rear chain instead of having a spring clip is riveted up.

Now a few words about the actual races. As many are aware, a race can be easily won or lost on the speed of pit work. You might expect from this that Craig stands over the Norton team and makes them rehearse and rehearse; certainly having seen their pit work I imagined that this might have been so, but Craig told me no, the riders had done it so many times before that it was almost automatic.

I have learned too that the trio we have come to know so well, when in for a fill-up do not ask questions. If the race is a continental one Joe says who will be first, where the rider who is filling up is lying, and who is just behind. In the TT this is done by the rider's pit attendant. Therefore there is no need for asking questions, and moreover the riders have long since ceased to waste time saying what conditions are like on the Mountain, they concentrate on seeing the particular tank for which they are responsible, and being men of sound sense they have come into their pits with bottom gear engaged, the magneto control suitably retarded, and filler caps undone all with the idea of saving seconds in re-fuelling and in getting away again. Seconds count; at least two races have been won this year by less than ten seconds and I am speaking not of riders in the same team but on different makes of machine. Imagine the anxieties of the team manager during a race. Picture his staring at those scoreboards, making mental calculations, wondering what if any-

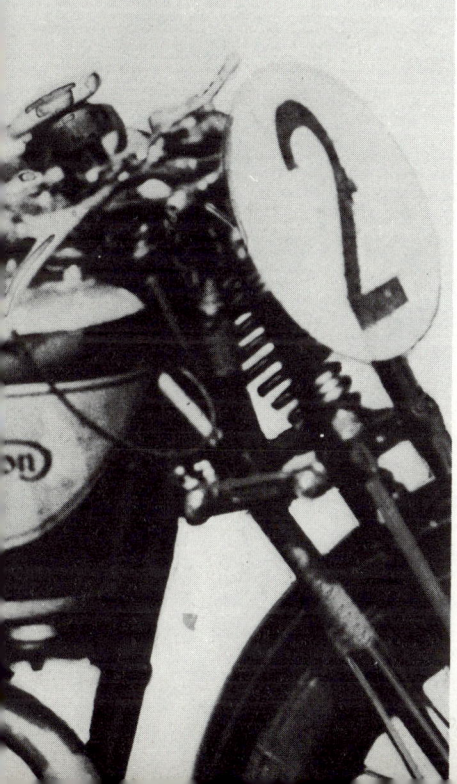

The famous partnership. Jimmy Guthrie receives the characteristic handshake from Joe Craig after the former's 1934 Junior TT win

thing will break. But Joe Craig is a phlegmatic type, and in any case how anxious he is on the day depends on how successful that work of his over the winter has been.

When it is all over there is the question of getting ready for the next race. If it is the TT the machines are hurried back to the works, stripped, examined with only two days in which to see to everything, and then off they go to the Continent for the series of big European races. There is never time in between these events for any serious work. Every week a different country is entered, with its Customs on the way in and on the way out, its languages, money, hotels and dozens of other worries for the team manager to see to and to solve. And then Joe Craig can think about his annual holiday, though with the Ulster so early these days even that may have to be taken 'when and how'.

The Work's racing models for 1934 incorporated hairpin valve-springs for the first time. On Guthrie's and Simpson's machines experimental megaphone exhaust systems were used, also two plug heads and twin spark magnetos. All the TT engines in outward appearance took on a more massive look with very deep cooling-fins around the cylinder barrel. Two ribs were cast onto the crankcase to assist in cooling the oil during its circulation.

The now familiar bolt-through tanks were also introduced.

Tyre sizes slightly altered: Senior models $3\frac{1}{2}$ inches section rear. Junior models $3\frac{1}{4}$ inches rear. Front tyres were of 3 inches section, of ribbed pattern on the front wheels of both machines.

Stanley Woods had left the Norton Team at end of 1933. The official Nortons were to be raced by Jimmy Guthrie, Walter Handley, Jimmy Simpson, Charlie Dodson. TT results: Guthrie and Simpson, first and second in the Senior, with Stanley Woods making fastest lap at 80.49mph on his Husqvarna. Guthrie and Simpson took first and second place again in the Junior race.

The last year of racing for Jimmy Simpson, the maker and breaker of lap records, whose only TT win was the Lightweight of 1934 on a Rudge. However Jimmy went out in a blaze of glory with wins in the 350cc class of the Belgian, German, Swiss and Ulster Grands Prix. He also won the 500cc class of the Swiss Grand Prix and Dutch TT.

In the Grand Prix d'Europe at Assen in Holland Jimmy Guthrie retired after his back wheel had slid from under him on a corner, resulting in his machine ploughing through the straw mattresses at this point, and then falling on him, and in consequence he suffered a broken arm and slight concussion. Demeuter, FN, won.

In the German Grand Prix, Otto Ley on his forced induction DKW two-stroke had won the Senior race after

the only Norton representative Walter Rusk had retired. In the Senior class of the Belgian Grand Prix new boys to the Norton Team, but old hands at the racing game, Walter Handley and Charlie Dodson were first and second.

The wiry schoolmaster from Radlett John 'Crasher' White won his first continental road race, the Dieppe Grand Prix, on his 500cc Norton. 'Crasher' could only be described as a character, and a member of the Cambridge University Auto Club 'The Quacks'. John White was a regular Brooklands performer, always wearing long stockings and brogues in preference to racing boots. He was a very fierce and determined rider and very, very unlike the prima donnas of the present day who more or less demand a circuit to be relaid before deigning to take saddle. An example of the type of courageous rider White was may be gleaned from the report in *Motor Cycling* June 1934 in which the full details of the Dieppe Grand Prix were published.

Song of the 'Quacks'. Malcolm Muir (centre), J H Fell, Jock Forbes (in cap), John White

'Due to the heat, the corner at Maison Blanche was a sea of melting tar, many riders had fallen here, some with serious results. Once White did a beautiful slide on the wet tar and swept on grinning broadly.'

It is conceivably possible that 'Crasher's' Norton was a semi-works-supported machine, for he had shown himself to be a consistent Manx Grand Prix performer, and no doubt had caught the eye of Joe Craig as a potential factory rider, indeed when the 1934 Manx Grand Prix came along in September all those present at the pre-race assembly had remarked on the great similarity between White's model and those used by the official Norton team in the June races.

The Swastika was much in evidence on the arms of the brown-shirted troops at the International Six Days Trial held in the Bavarian Alps, everything conducted on very military lines. Germany first, and the runners-up Italy while Great Britain was third with Vic Brittain (348 Norton) in the British contingent.

At the Olympia Show.

The International models of 1934 were fitted with hairpin valve-springs.

The fishtail-type silencer was discarded in favour of one of circular section.

Gearboxes which had been almost entirely of Sturmey Archer manufacture, were now of Norton make, although most parts were still interchangeable. The TT type positive stop foot control was freely available on all models, although the earlier system of hand change could still be supplied if so required.

A central prop-stand was fitted in addition to the front and rear stands. Handlebars were rubber mounted.

Benito Mussolini shows interest in an 'Inter' Norton at the Milan Show of 1934. At this time British motorcycles were held in the highest esteem

Dennis Mansell, son of the managing director of Nortons, blasts his outfit up 'Fowlers Run' in the Streatham Trophy Trial. The racing mechanic Bill Mewis occupies the sidecar

For the Trials-riding enthusiast a Norton could be supplied with appropriate trials specification at an extra cost of five pounds sterling; this included a higher ground-clearance, obtained by means of a special frame. High level exhaust system, competition tyres, a narrow front fork and a low-ratio, trials gearbox. In addition there were chromium-plated rims, mud-guards and chain guard and other special features. The well proven cradle frame was now available on the International models plus the CS1, CJ and the ES2, the remainder of the range retaining the semi-loop type. There were no price increases of any importance.

To wind up the year Jimmy Guthrie broke two 500cc records, the fifty-kilometre and fifty-miles at Montlhéry track near Paris, on what was virtually a TT Norton, the only alterations being the placing of the saddle over the rear wheel (out and out Brooklands fashion), a larger fuel tank, and a streamlined aluminium cowl covering the major part of the steering head and front wheel. The compression ratio was raised to accept alcohol fuel.

The two records were particularly worthy achievements, for the actual surface at Montlhéry was smooth almost polished concrete and parts of the track on the steep banking which the sun had not reached even at 1.45pm were still coated with a film of ice. Added to this Guthrie had to contend with a twenty-mile per hour wind. In the opening months of 1935 one of the motorcycling journals carried out a road test of a Norton Big Four and semi-sports sidecar. The Big Four had always been the favourite of Pa Norton, indeed it was but an extension of his remarkable character – solid, well built and completely reliable. Even with the coming of the overhead-valve engine, the Big Four had remained an outstanding model, and 1935 found it still in a state of robust health and filling a definite niche, a side-valve machine designed for really hard work where more than one person was to be carried in solo or sidecar form

All the refinements that were appropriate to this model were fitted as a result of 'certain' tried and proven items in the TT and other races. Perhaps a little quaint however was the retention of the cast aluminium foot-boards on the big side-valve, instead of the more or less universally adopted footrests; indeed the test-rider had experienced some little difficulty in getting his right foot in the correct position in order to change gear with the foot change mechanism.

With a total of 22 stones of person aboard, the Big Four and sidecar had returned a mean maximum speed of 59mph on a top gear of 5.17 to 1, and its petrol consumption 52 miles per gallon at an average speed of 35mph. Oil consumption was 2,000mpg.

The test-rider further praised the superb steering and general handling, and that the machine could be ridden hands off without that usual front wheel wobble that is associated with sidecar machines at low speeds. The solid family man of the mid-'Thirties could choose no better, the big 633cc model could be relied upon to work day in day out, and just would not wear out.

A more lean and rakish-looking machine than the Norton TT job would be difficult to find, the right tool for the job, nothing superfluous about it – adequate comments indeed for the racing Nortons for the 1935 contests. There were secret internal modifications but these were to remain, for the time being, very hush-hush. What was known was that a different type of hairpin valve-spring was to be used in which its coils were tight up together instead of being clear of each other, this was said to have had the effect of eliminating valve-surge.

In order to steady the top part of the

Above: With swastika armband, Nazi Minister of Sport, Korpsführer Huhnlein, salutes Walter Rusk, winner of the 350cc class in the German Grand Prix, 1935. Joe Craig, his face hidden by the microphone cover, keeps his arms firmly at his side. Below: The moment when works DKW rider Winkler screamed his 250cc model past the Nortons on his way to a Lightweight win in the Swiss Grand Prix, Berne, 1935

engine, and thus reduce any vibration, two small diameter tubes, flattened at either end, were taken from the cylinder-head to a suitable position on the front down-tube, while the anchorage of the engine was modified further by the inclusion of two holding plates which were placed at the highest available point of the crankcase.

Yet another improvement related to the drive side mainshaft bearing which now was of the triple-roller type, secured by a large nut which screwed directly onto the sleeve of the bearing and pulled the inner shoulder of the sleeve tight up to its face on the inside of the crankcase.

Both Junior and Senior models now had an increased fuel capacity of four gallons and the oil tanks contained four pints of oil. Formerly the handlebars were of one inch diameter, they were now reduced to seven eighths of an inch, but were made of a heavier gauge metal.

The brake drums remained at seven inches in diameter both back and front, but were surrounded by aluminium fins, three on each drum, to assist in cooling these very hard-working items.

A large milled adjustor was placed high up on the front fork blade, where it could be reached by the rider during the course of a race, thus allowing brake adjustment to be made while the machine was on the move.

The 1935 Works Nortons were raced by Jimmy Guthrie, Walter Rusk, and in certain races John 'Crasher' White and J G Duncan were to be additions to the team, and in the usual pre-TT try-out Irish races the Nortons secured yet more wins, but with the actual June races in the Isle of Man, the situation was a little different. The Junior race had been fought and won with Guthrie, Rusk and White finishing first, second and third, the pretty camshaft Velocettes harrying them in no uncertain manner, but Stanley Woods, now riding for the Italian Moto Guzzi concern, was about to break the Norton dominance of the Senior TT even though his win from Jimmy Guthrie was only by a whisker of four seconds: now of course very much history, yet still inclined to bring out the more demonstrative side of the older student of motorcycle racing when the Woods/Guthrie duel is under discussion. In but a few lines the plot was as follows. As Guthrie was approaching Ramsey on his seventh and last lap his signalling station held out their boards, indicating that he now could take it a little easier, as Woods (wide angle twin Moto Guzzi), was just completing his penultimate lap and was in about the Governor's

Bridge area, some eighteen miles distant from the Norton rider. Woods had started some time after Guthrie and therefore his present road position was quite in the order of things. But with Wood's own secret signalling stations around the course and an absolute masterly piece of acting by his Guzzi pit attendants who made every sign of preparation for a fuel stop by the Irishman, the news was quickly telegraphed to Guthrie's Ramsey station, with the consequent instruction to ease off. Stanley had no intention of stopping for fuel and made a last minute but well calculated spurt. The rest, as previously mentioned, is history. On with the Continental round with the Norton Team cleaning up the two classes of the Swiss Grand Prix, although in the 350cc event run concurrently with the 250cc class DKW

two-stroke rider Winkler had actually screamed past the Norton Junior machines when securing his Lightweight win. There followed the Dutch TT at the Van Drenthe circuit with Guthrie taking the honours in the 500cc class and Rusk doing likewise in the 350cc race. Poor 'Crasher' had retired with a broken fork spring. The wins continued both in the German Grand Prix at Chemnitz, pronounced Kemnitz, and in the 'Belgian'.

At Brooklands, Charles Mortimer Senior won the Senior Mountain Championship on his 500cc Norton, while Harold Daniell rode his 350 model into first place in the Junior event, even greater days were but a few years away for Harold in his association with the Norton marque.

Still, in those palmy days of 1935, the world's fastest road race, the Ulster Grand Prix, Senior class was won by Jimmy Guthrie at over ninety miles per hour, even after having taken a tumble in an attempt to avoid a fallen team-

Left to right, Joe Craig, Gilbert Smith and Bill Mansell hover over the 'Inter' at the 1935 Olympia show

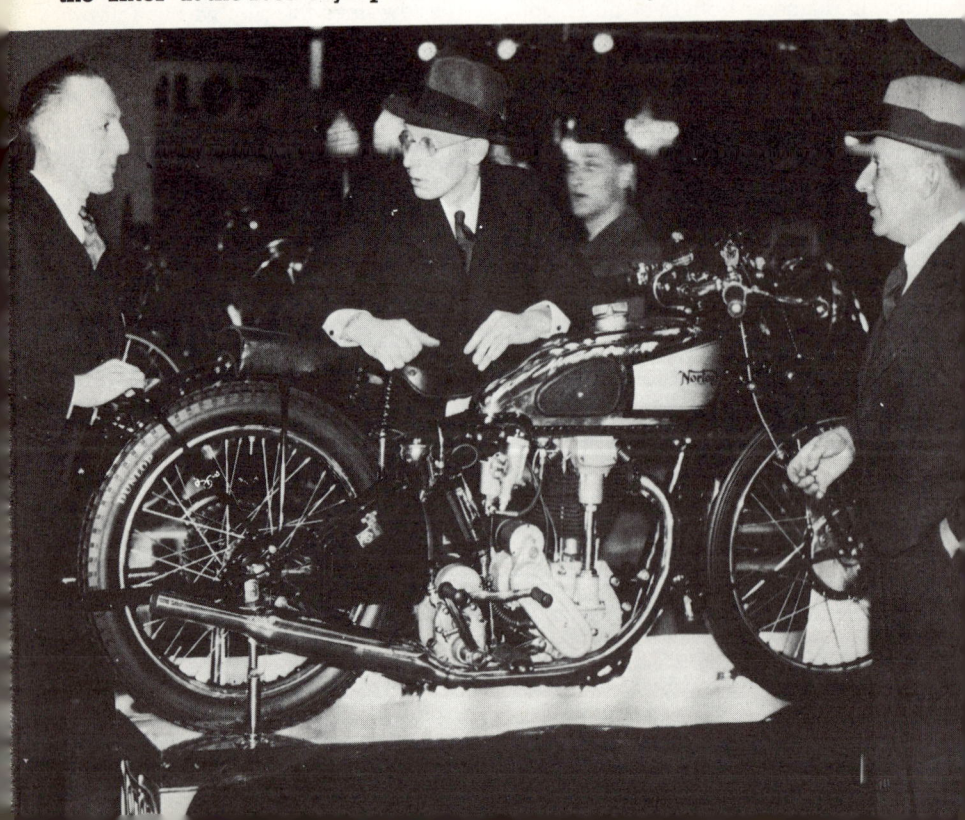

mate during the course of the race. The Velocettes were now showing their speed potential and had won the 350cc race, with Norton's Duncan and White occupying third and fourth places.

For the Senior race, twenty-one starters were mounted on ten different makes of machine, there were five Nortons, two DKW two-strokes, to be ridden by Otto Ley and H P Muller, plus representatives of New Imperial, FN, Royal Enfield, Rudge, Velocette, Vincent HRD factories – a sole HHE, and a Moto Guzzi.

As the starting flag was lowered Guthrie and Rusk shot into the lead, and maintained these positions for the first lap, not that the opposition were very far behind. On the second circuit Rusk fell at Aldergrove, and Guthrie, in an attempt to avoid running over Rusk, crashed also. With a badly bent handlebar Jimmy got going again however, although he was now down in fourth position. On lap three the Norton Ace well and truly opened up his machine and in so doing was to make fastest lap of the day at 95.35mph. Jimmy continued his furious pace until having regained the lead, wisely decided to ease off to a degree. Meanwhile retirements were coming thick and fast with Stanley Woods on his Guzzi passing from the scene on the sixth lap. Other 'cracks' were falling by the wayside.

After nine laps Guthrie had won, a spirited piece of riding if ever there was.

ULSTER GRAND PRIX. Senior race 1935
(Grand Prix of Europe)

1 J Guthrie (490 Norton)	90.98mph
2 Rene Milhoux (FN)	89.11mph
3 Arthur Tyler (Velo)	87.69mph
4 Ted Mellors (FN)	86.26mph
5 Ginger Wood (New Imp)	83.26mph
6 H P Muller (DKW)	77.54mph

RECORD LAP

J Guthrie (490 Norton)	95.35mph

Some of the works Nortons at this period appeared to be fitted with aluminium wheel rims, although instead of being left in their natural bright finish, these rims were painted black.

The International models could now be obtained with racing specification, with the result that unofficially, such models so fettled were referred to as Manx Nortons.

The petrol tanks on all machines in the range, with the exception of the 'Inters', were of new design, being three quarters of an inch deeper and half an inch wider at the nose thus increasing the capacity to two and three quarter gallons. The side-valve models were fitted with a new aluminium valve-cover of very neat appearance, with two cut-aways at the top to allow the valve guides (fitted with grease-nipples) to be greased without the necessity of having to remove the cover. On the overhead-valve models 18, 20 and ES2, the cylinder holding down bolts were now extended from the crankcase to the top of the cylinder head as on the Internationals, while the cam profiles were ground with an improved contour.

Again the Inters were available with their cylinder-heads in light alloy for which an extra charge of £5.0.0 was made. For all models a Lucas mag/dyno lighting set was an extra at £5.10.0 for solos and £6.0.0 for sidecar machines so equipped.

While the editor and staff of the motorcycling journals wished their readers the compliments of the Christmas season, young Jones plotted and pleaded with Pater to let him have an 'Inter', justifying all with – 'Smith Major has one, and he has a Brooklands 'can', and a super leather coat, and an absolutely smashing pair of Lance Gaye goggles. He rides awfully well, very safe you know, and his house master rides one and and . . .'. 'We will see my boy, we will see'. Those wonderful 'Thirties, at least as far as motor and motorcycle sport was concerned. True there were twinges of uneasiness in certain parts of Europe politically, but the sophisticated racing machinery in the hands of the world's greatest riders, created an air of excitement.

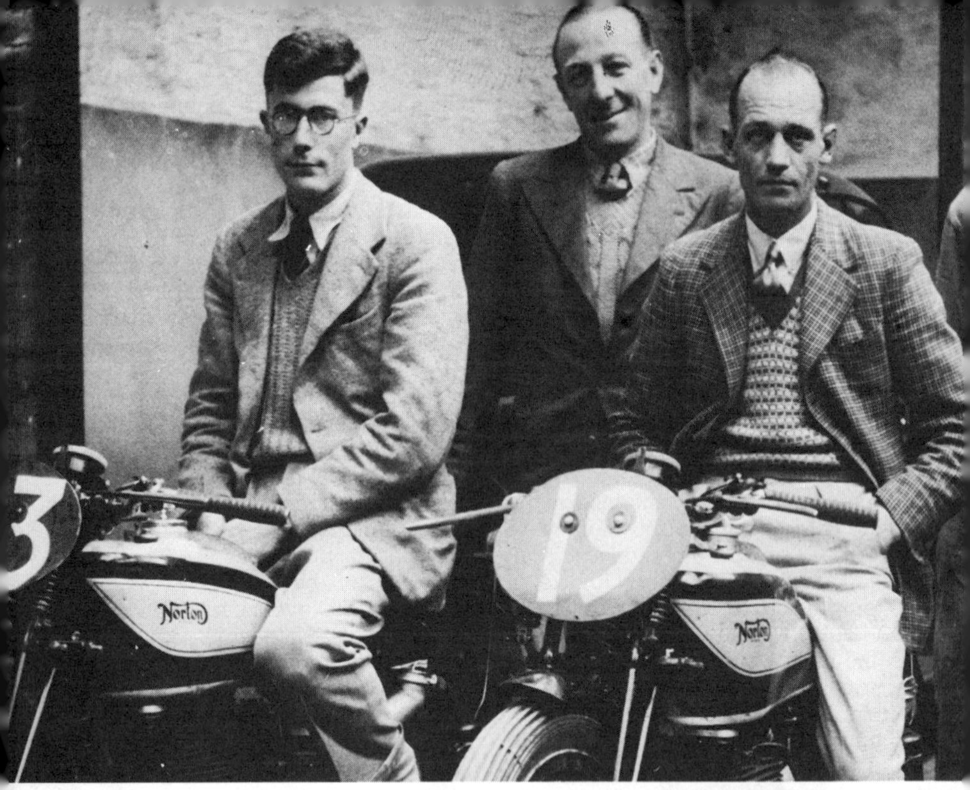
3
Norton
19
Norton

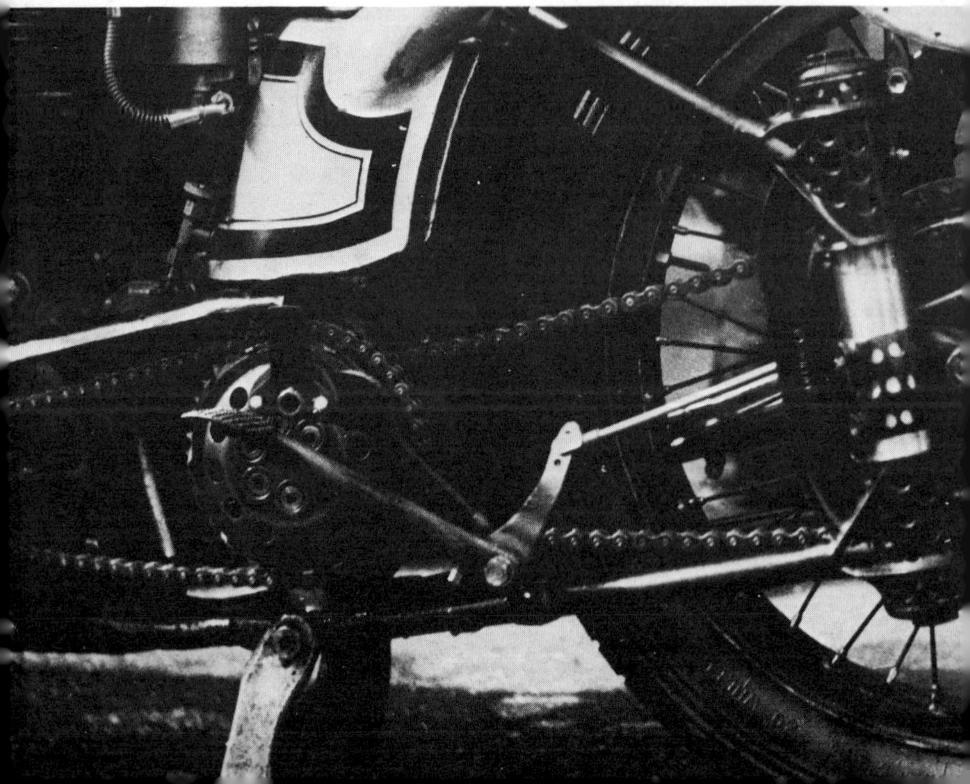

Formidable team (from left) White, Craig, Guthrie, Mewis and Frith

The 'Twenties were charactered years, but now perhaps five or six works teams would take their place on the starting grid, each with a good chance of victory although, one must hasten to add, reliability still remained the outstanding quality of the British Norton, and Joe Craig's 'boys' disciplined so well in the art of Grand Prix racing possessed a head start over the wilder temperament of their more flamboyant continental rivals.

Prior to the hustle and bustle of the racing season of 1936, Peter Chamberlain ('Cyclops' of *Motorcycling*) interviewed Jimmy Guthrie at his family garage business in Hawick. Here was Jimmy, in a well tailored suit, no trendy side whiskers and other phoney gimmicks, taking a little time off from business to talk about the game he loved. A great physical training enthusiast, Jimmy would ride from his home to the Edinburgh gymnasium on, of course, a replica TT Norton. Apparently he used to blind a bit between the two places, resulting in the officials of two railway stations which he passed en route, making a practice of timing him over the stretch between the two stations. This worried Jimmy when he learnt about it, for as he mentioned to 'Cyclops' – 'In the event of my meeting with an accident, witnesses would be called, and no doubt the words "excessive speed" would be uttered.' Fast riding on the road was therefore called to a halt. Guthrie, a keen gardener when time permitted, was then thirty-nine years old, married, with two children, and contrary to 'Ixion's' belief that twenty-five was the terminating age for motorcycle road racing, Jimmy was in his very prime, indeed considered to be one of the world's number one riders.

The appearance of the heavy plunger suspension on the works Nortons in 1936. Note the aluminium wheel rim hiding beneath a coat of black paint

Needless to say, Bracebridge Street models won both Senior and Junior events in the TT with Stanley Woods, mounted on the big 500cc Velocette preventing a one-two-three Norton victory, by riding into second position behind Guthrie and in front of Freddie Frith, Freddie having taken over from Walter Rusk who was ousted from the racing scene until 1938 with a broken wrist.

In the Junior TT Jimmy Guthrie was stopped and disqualified for an alleged breach of the rules. At Hillberry he was forced to stop, for the rear chain had jumped the sprockets, and it was

The solid 500cc ES 2 of Henry Herbert Smith, showing every evidence of its daily round

alleged that he had received a push in order to re-start, from a well meaning marshal. Guthrie protested that he had not asked for any assistance, it being quite contrary to the rules, and the allegation was subsequently disproved. Jimmy was therefore recognised as a finisher (he had continued after the Hillberry incident) but the ACU would not disturb the already announced finishing order. Freddie Frith won the race at over eighty miles an hour, with John White in second place.

At the Swiss Grand Prix of 1936, the sprung rear wheel had made its first appearance on the official Norton entries. Joe Craig insisted that it was purely experimental, although it was a logical step for many of the foreign racing machines possessed some form of rear

suspension, in order to eliminate what is described as back wheel-hop, particularly on bumpy circuits. The arrangement consisted of a pair of pistons, or plungers, housed in a machined casting that was attached to the frame, one on each side of the rear wheel. To these plungers the housing of the wheel spindle was rigidly bolted, centrally. Compression springs were positioned above and below the plungers. On the 350 model no system of damping was employed, but on the Senior machine a hydraulic medium was incorporated to resist the tendency for the suspension to bottom under severe stress. The whole assembly was immensely robust and the wheel was kept well and truly in line. At the front end of these works Nortons, the large barrel spring set

within the girder forks, now had, in place of the former rigid bottom anchorage, a ball and socket assembly which permitted the spring to seat itself automatically, and to prevent bowing when under compression, the cause of many fork-spring failures. Surprisingly Nortons had not suffered at all badly from this complaint over their racing years, it is an indication of the complete thoroughness however that Joe Craig practised in the preparation of the racing machines.

Following Guthrie's Junior and Senior wins in the 'Swiss', the Norton star said of the new suspension, 'I have never had a more comfortable day's racing, and it was easy to see that the machine handled perfectly.'

Supercharging was rearing its interesting head, chiefly on the continent, the Germans and Italians being quick to develop this system of forced induction. The blown BMWs ridden by Otto Ley and Karl Gall had completely vanquished the normally aspirated Nortons in the Swedish Grand Prix: the writing was on the wall.

The private owner was now asking that the famous spring heel be made generally available. Nortons replied with an emphatic 'No' to this demand, stating that until they had perfect confidence in the fitting and had conducted tests under full touring conditions they were not prepared to introduce any form of rear suspension to the general motorcycling public. The sporting Norton rider could now purchase an aluminium cylinder barrel and head for his Model CS1 or CJ for the extra sum of £5.0.0.

Old Pa Norton's policy so many years before, that racing improves the breed; so true, for Henry Herbert Smith of Surbiton, bank clerk in the City, could ride his model ES2 day after day to his place of business, confident in the knowledge that beneath him was a Norton machine possessing all the excellent and reliable qualities that had been put to the greatest of tests on the race tracks of the world.

WINDS OF CHANGE

The first 'double knocker' unit, 1937

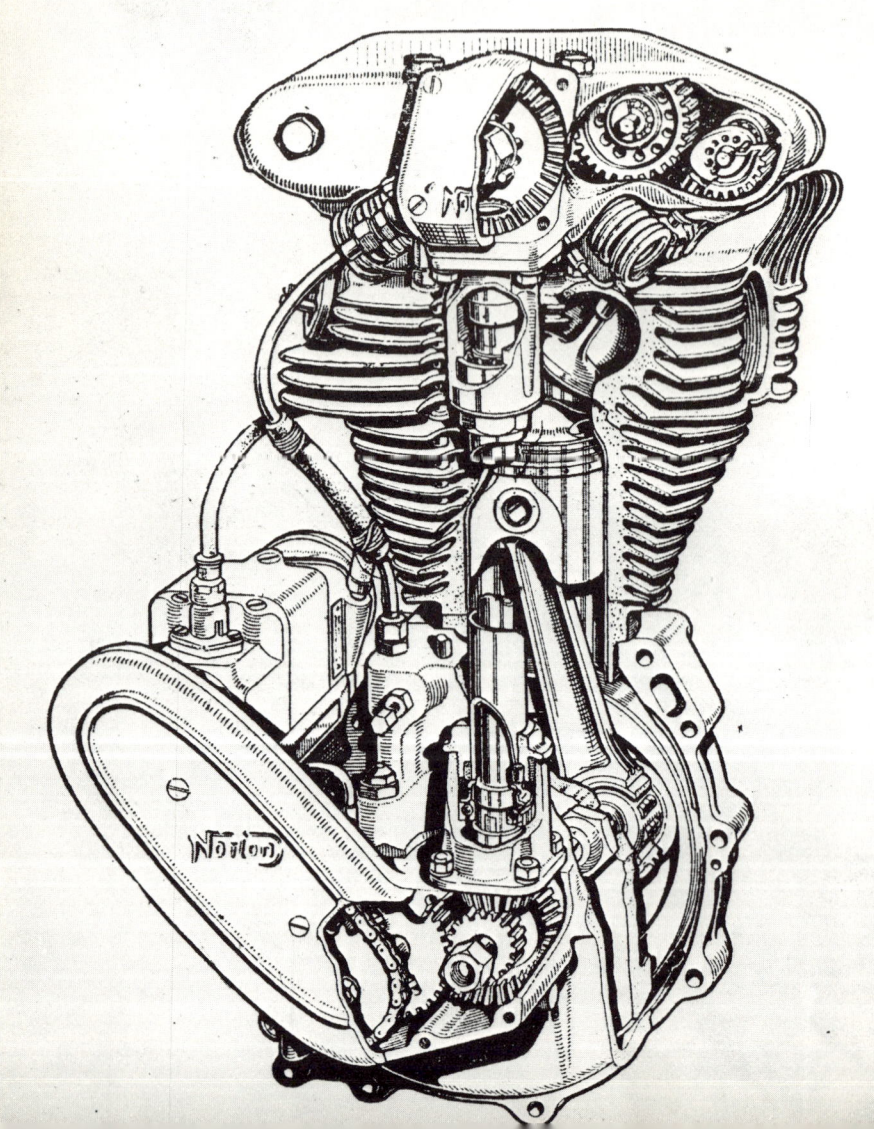

Now came what was surely the saddest year for Norton Motors Ltd since the passing of 'The Old Man' in 1925. In August 1937 Jimmy Guthrie had met his death in the German Grand Prix on the Hohenstein – Ernstthal circuit at Chemnitz in Saxony. Before an estimated crowd of 200,000 race enthusiasts, a furious battle had developed between Karl Gall on his supercharged BMW and the dashing Scot, in the Senior event. The BMW was undoubtedly the faster machine and was leading Guthrie by a small margin; perhaps the Norton's superior road-holding and greater skill of its jockey could yet oust Gall from the lead ? Riding like a soul possessed Guthrie hung on grimly to the Teutonic tail, cornering at frightening angles in his dramatic attempt to overhaul the German. The moment came for a do or die effort when Gall overshot his pit when coming in to refuel his thirsty machine, and in consequence wasted valuable time in wheeling backwards to his anxious pit attendant. This incident left the Norton star in the lead, but alas for but a very brief period, because on the final lap, when heeled over for a slight curve before the finish, Guthrie's Norton went out of control and poor Jimmy crashed heavily, sustaining injuries that were to prove fatal a short time later, thus providing a somewhat hollow victory for Karl Gall. It is said that the Saxon race are without sentiment other than for horses, dogs and war comrades lost: however Britain's Jimmy Guthrie was adored by the German spectators, and they turned away not knowing how to contain their grief. The sting had gone from the Norton camp, their Superman had gone to rest.

With Guthrie's death, an era had passed; admittedly there were at least three men of star quality who could be relied upon to uphold the Norton banner, but the continental rival firms were now producing considerably faster racing motorcycles even if their road-holding qualities left much to be desired. 1937 was to see the last of Norton supremacy for a time.

The racing Nortons were the last word in non-supercharged single-cylinder design, with the introduction of the double overhead-camshaft engines for 1937, the first major change in engine layout since late 1930. The rockers were now eliminated and replaced by a separate camshaft above each valve, and operating them through short tappets, the valve-springs were still exposed, but the finning, both on the cylinder head and barrel, had now assumed very large proportions and the very attractive 'square' head came into being. Edgar Franks had designed a new type of front brake drum of conical shape which gave much greater rigidity to the braking surface. It is interesting to note that revolution counters were not regularly used on these works racing models, indeed managing director Bill Mansell had gone as far as to say that the riders had managed sufficiently well in the past without these instruments, and it was doubtful if they would appear on the TT Nortons. There must have been a change of mind however, for personal memories of the pre-war TT models are clear enough to recall that these Nortons were certainly fitted with rev-counters, with their drive taken either from the timing cover, or in some cases from one of the camshafts.

With the TT races, Guthrie, Frith and White scooped the first three places in the Junior race, but in the Friday's Senior event Jimmy Guthrie retired on the fifth lap whereupon a battle-royal commenced between Freddie Frith and Stanley Woods (500cc Velocette) who on the sixth lap were dead-heating for first place.

Frith eventually won and in so doing made history, as Jimmy Simpson had been wont to do in the past, by recording the first lap at over 90mph. The great Norton Trials rider Jack Williams rode what could be described as an experimental model in the TT; it featured a single overhead-camshaft engine employing coil-valve springs, the valve gear being totally enclosed. The unit was housed in the conventional spring

Far right: Jimmy Guthrie corners on the new twin overhead camshaft Norton in the Leinster '200' races, May 1937. Note the conical front hub assembly. **Right:** Engine changes on the standard models in Coronation year. The overhead valve unit with totally enclosed valve gear and sloping push rod tubes. **Below:** The side–valve Model 16H of 490cc

heel frame, the Norton policy being that, should the machine come through the race successfully, then it would form the basis of 'next year's' standard Manx replica.

Harold Daniell, mentioned on one or two occasions earlier in the book, had given a quite remarkable performance in both the Senior and Junior races on his Lancefield-tuned, privately owned Nortons, by securing fifth place in both events. It was quite natural therefore that he should find himself a member of the official Norton team, and during the latter part of 1937, this in fact happened.

It is inevitable that any author must take stock of time and space, but steeped in the magic of the Norton history it is with some reluctance that it is necessary to pare down to the basic details only, the final sequence of events leading up to the outbreak of the Second World War.

Although by 1938 Joe Craig, Norton's remarkable development engineer, who incidentally had no letters whatsoever after his name and had extracted just about fifty brake horsepower from the petrol-benzole fed TT Norton 500cc engine, realised only too well that something would have to be done further to fight off the continental menace, as it was referred to. It is known that Craig was not averse to copying other manufacturers' designs if he considered them to be efficient, and perhaps therefore the similarity – framewise – between the 1938 Nortons and the German BMW racers may have some significance.

By May 1938 Nortons announced the

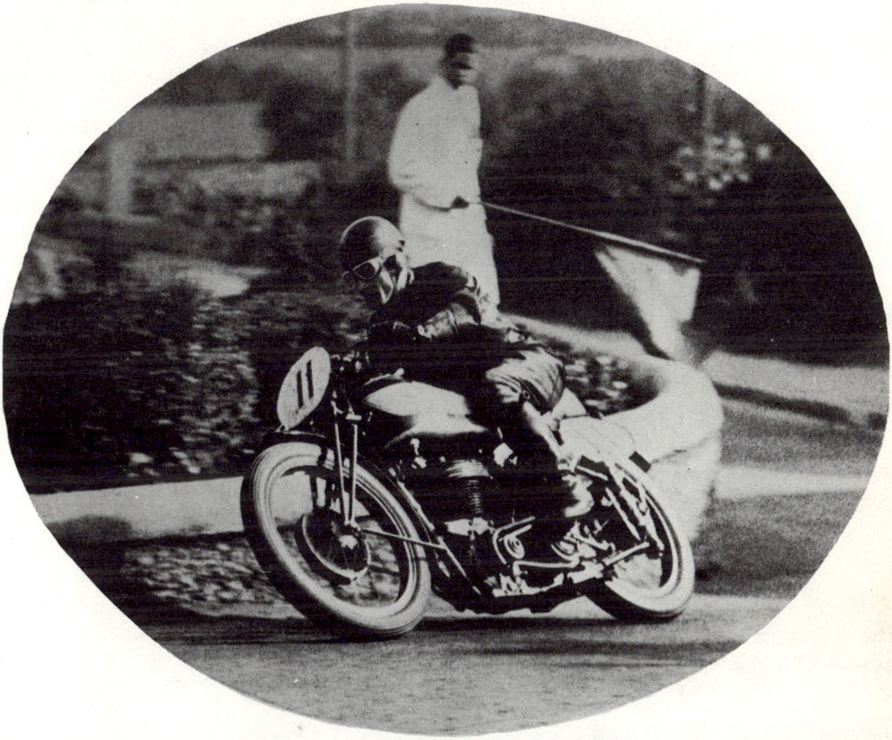
11

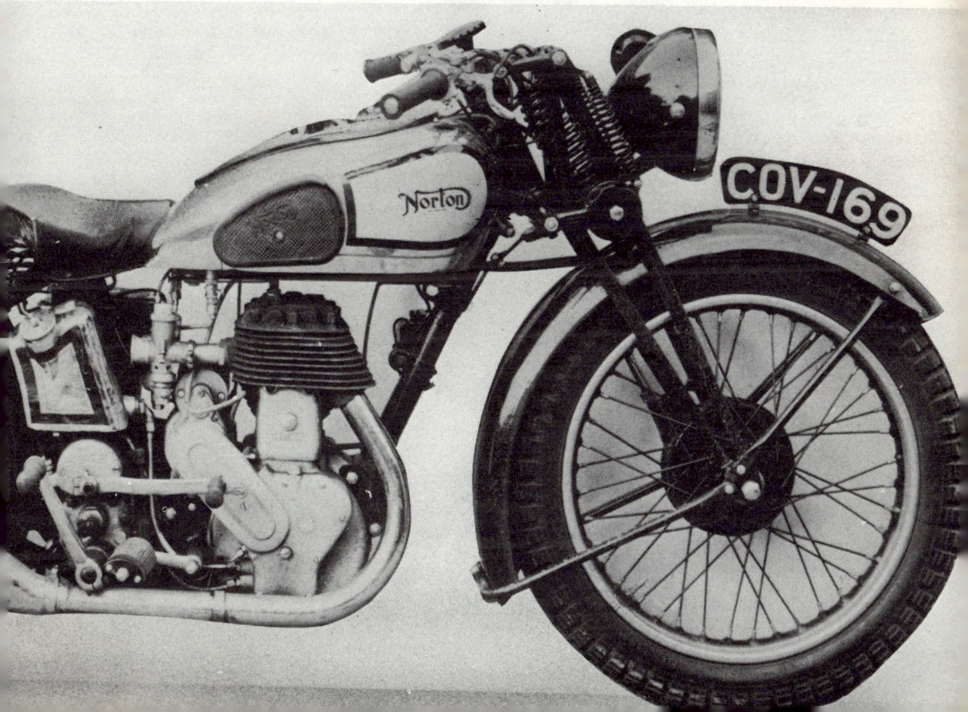
Norton
COV-169

introduction of what they called their 'Entirely New Racing Mounts'. It was usual for the eyes of the enthusiast to be centered on Norton machines in the TT races, thus those glances were keener than ever. From stem to stern the Norton TT machines were new, although the makers continued to pin their faith to the single-cylinder overhead-camshaft type of engine that had proved so successful in the past.

It is difficult to know where to start in describing the new models, but probably the power unit would be a good point to begin.

Firstly the bore and stroke dimensions were altered, giving the engines much shorter strokes (both 350s and 500s) than had previously been the case. The double overhead-camshaft was exactly the same as in the previous year's engines, but the valves were larger. A considerable modification to

The German supercharged BMW, ridden by Jock West. They were a headache for Joe Craig

the outward appearance of the engines had been made however. The finning on the cylinder barrel and head was even deeper still, and in the case of the Senior model the barrel had its base sunk three quarters of an inch deeper into the crankcase. To achieve this the crankcase had to be re-designed and the upper half was carried high around the cylinder. One result of this was a much firmer engine mounting in which the plates embraced more of the crankcase. Additionally there was now some deep finning on the forward upper part of the crankcase.

The bottom part of the lower bevel chamber had been raised somewhat in order that the exhaust pipe tucked below it should have greater ground clearance. The fuel and oil tanks, always sure seducers to the Norton enthusiast, were possibly just a little more rounded at the corners than before, but the oil tanks now possessed that familiar long neck extending way back alongside the rear wheel on the 'pit' or near side. A new innovation

was an oil cooler, mounted above the gearbox.

The compression ratios on both Junior and Senior models were 'upped' to a slight degree, and the engines breathed through a large-bore, remote needle Amal carburettor, in which the float chamber was mounted rigidly with the main body, but the main instrument was mounted flexibly by means of a rubber connection to the induction pipe.

Both the clutch and foot change mechanism were as before, but the four-speed gear-boxes now possessed, in addition to the top mounting, a further location to a platform welded to each part of the lower frame tubes.

The frame was almost entirely new. A similar layout to former designs was used in the main part, but instead of the usual cradle, continuous tubes were taken from the base of the front down-tube to the rear wheel. In the rear suspension some modifications were to be found, the seat and chain stays were joined by bracing tubes located just in front of the spring housings. At a first glance the rear suspension appeared much the same as before, but this was far from the case. Running from the rear of the chain stays to the rear of the seat stays (the ends of which were wide apart) was a fixed tubular guide. Around this fitted a long sleeve which was integral with the rear fork ends. Outside this sleeve, and above and below the fork ends were the upper and lower springs, encased in telescopic tubes which were retained by the springs. Through the inner guide a long bolt passed which retained the whole assembly to the seat and chain stays. Under the influence of road shocks the wheel fork ends and their sleeves rode up the guide tube and compressed the upper springs. On the return, movement was checked by the lower springs.

The Italian four-cylinder liquid cooled Gilera Rondine. Both this and the BMW were at least twenty-five miles per hour faster than the non-supercharged Norton

The whole assembly was much neater and more fully enclosed than was the old design, while the new arrangement of fork ends and sleeves gave a greater lateral rigidity.

The front end of the machine was very different from any previous Norton model, and the forks were designed on a similar principle to the rear suspension. Two very large diameter tubes were used, rigidly mounted to the steering head, and sliding into these were the fork legs, there being main and rebound springs situated between the two assemblies, but no damping. These early forks were certainly an advance in certain respects over the former girder pattern, but their actual movement was very little over two inches.

A pleasing near-side view of the 'entirely new' Norton, as ridden by Freddie Frith in the Ulster Grand Prix. The long seat and rear footrests were not standard on these machines

In addition to the conical front hub, the rear wheel was similarly fitted and was worked by a short cable from the brake pedal, in place of a rod as previously.

Writing about the new Nortons, an observer in the motorcycling Press said: 'This then is the story of the 1938 racers, but it is a story that is only half told. Its end will be written on the twisting $37\frac{1}{2}$-mile Isle of Man course and on the famous continental road-race circuits. It is a tale which is sure to prove interesting and the Norton Company and their riders can be relied upon to make it dramatic'. There was drama indeed, for Freddie Frith, who, during practice for the North West 200 expressed the opinion that his new model possessed considerably more urge and really marvellous road-holding qualities, was to slide to earth on a very wet and slippery surface during the actual race. Drama indeed that responsibility then fell on 'Crasher' White's shoulders who, piloting a sister

machine to Frith's was to fall and retire also. Perhaps a little ironical is the fact therefore that Jack Moore was to win the race on a virtually standard racing Norton that was at least two years old.

In a more suburban setting, Londoners at their own very testing little circuit at Crystal Palace were watching the impressive sidecar antics of Jack Surtees, (father of the remarkable John) on his 596cc Norton outfit. Just how many top sidecar men were using the big 600cc motor in the pre-war period is not known with accuracy, but a personal memory of the two closing years of the decade, would put the number at between five or six. These Norton 'Bigger Bangers' as they were affectionately called later, were not really in any way connected with the revised pushrod-operated overhead-valve Model 19 of similar capacity, although it is conceivably possible that Kim Collett's original outfit at Syston in the very early 'thirties may have been based on the '19'. These 'Bigger

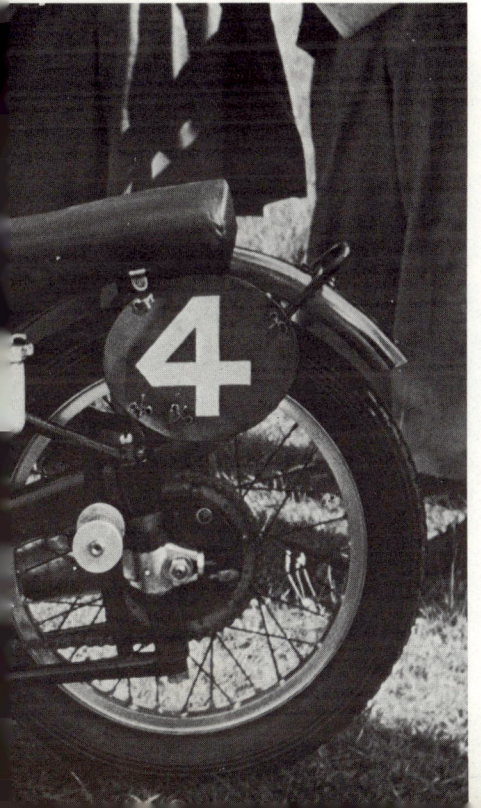

Bangers' always appear to be some mystery Norton device when they come under discussion, it would be perhaps wise therefore to bring them a little more into the light. Bracebridge Street never listed the particular engine for sale to the public, for the simple reason that it really did not exist as a production job. In conversation with both Cyril Quantrill and Arthur Horton recently, the latter being the most successful and indeed most professional Norton sidecar racer in the immediate pre-war period, the following information was kindly given. The Norton works produced two versions of a 596cc single overhead-camshaft engine, (82mm x 113mm) one in International, and one in Manx form, there being some subtle differences internally between the two units. Quantrill suggested that roughly a dozen of each were manufactured, the frames being of stouter construction, and having a large vertical 'kink' in the upper frame tube in order to accept the considerably taller engine. It appears that the 'Inters' were primarily built for the leading Trials sidecar men of the period, while the hotter Manx model was more strictly suited to sidecar road racing. As several Manx '600s' were doing battle in passenger machine races in the immediate post-war era, it is surprising to learn that few, if any still exist. Cyril Quantrill will be remembered as the well known *Motor Cycling* journalist who had Norton build him a special 'cammy' 600 from a number of parts that were laying about at Bracebridge Street, and hitched to a TT Hughes sidecar; this 'hairy' combination with Quantrill a-puffing at his pipe could see off most solos on the uncluttered roads of the late 'Forties. Arthur Horton with passenger Les Seals, were practically unbeatable on most British road courses, and their performances at Donington were quite exceptional, in fact this sidecar team were first to adopt the continental style of modern racing in which the passenger would lie flat on his belly, with his head facing forwards in the 'chair', to engage only in the smoothest of acrobatics when fast corners were to be negotiated. It was a system frowned on by the British critics at first as being wildly dangerous as Seals' face was sometimes no more than two or three inches from the ground, when leaning out for 'left handers'. But when the professional-looking pair took their six hundred spring heel, but girder forked outfit to the 1938 Swiss Grand Prix and knocked the continental opposition for six, no more criticism was heard.

There have been many sensational races and TT victories, indeed this is what makes motorcycle racing one of the greatest sports, although, sadly, not recognised by those who have never tried to understand what it is all about. Among the list of these sensational events was the Senior TT of 1938.

The prettiest of all racing 350s, the

The Arthur Horton/Les Seals combination (No 58) showing their professional technique at Redgate Corner, Donington Park, 1938

Velocette with Stanley Woods 'up' had won the Junior race earlier in the week, with another Hall Green product in the hands of Ted Mellors in second place. Freddie Frith on the 'new' Norton coming home third. However Harold Daniell's victory in the Senior is now history.

Harold was of course a member of the official Norton team, but as the works machines were late in arriving in the Island for practice, Daniell was using his older Donington 500 in order to get in some necessary laps. Just after Balla-craine he got into a slide at about 90mph and caught a stone wall with the inside footrest causing him to crash badly enough to need hospital treatment. Being a particularly tough individual Harold was fit enough for the Junior race in which he finished fifth with a partially seized motor on his new Norton. If Joe Craig was at this stage feeling, justifiably, downcast over the apparent lack of form his models were showing, the Senior race was to put the smile back into his face. In 1946

Harold gave a very interesting talk to members of the Ravensbury MCC which he titled *Twenty Years of Racing,* and his account of that 1938 Senior ride is of great interest. One could do no better therefore than present this drama in his own words.

'On the opening lap of the Senior race I did not flatten the motor out until it was thoroughly warmed up, I was afraid of a repetition of Monday's seizure and as a result my position was fourth at the end of the circuit. By now I was getting used to the monster [Harold had made it quite clear during an earlier try out that it was far too heavy, and he cared not for the telescopic forks] but I received no signals at Ramsey and only got a request for more speed each time I passed the pits. At the end of the third lap I stopped for fuel and oil and learnt that I was in third position and not going fast enough.

'I was now riding all out and the only way to improve my speed was to thrash the motor. I had been driving on the rev counter and knowing that these instruments are far from reliable, I decided to drive by ''feel''. This proved successful and at lap six my signal at Ramsey was a large W with –5 underneath. I was pleased to receive a signal at Ramsey at last, I was in the race after all, but the W meant that Woods (500 Velocette) was leading, and that was not going to be very popular with the Bracebridge Street Firm. I wondered where team mate Freddie Frith was lying, actually we were dead-heated in second place. On my last lap past the pits my signal was 2nd–3 with frantic waving to supplement the sign. Actually I had a lead of five seconds at this point but as Woods' number was 30 and mine 15 the signal referred to my position at Ramsey. On the last lap Ramsey signal was 1–5 and I nearly fell off with excitement. I calculated that now I was in the lead and had only to maintain my speed and concentrate on avoiding mistakes and then it would be in the bag, actually the final lap proved to be my fastest, and is the present lap record of twenty-four

Harold Daniell at his Forest Hill premises a few weeks after the sensational TT ride. The record lap was in fact 1.6 seconds slower than shown

minutes, fifty-two point six seconds – 91mph.'

Behind Woods in third place rode Freddie Frith on the other works Norton. It was not in fact until 1950 that that sensational lap record speed was beaten, when once again Nortons, overcoming the poorer quality Pool petrol as opposed to the pre-war petrol/benzole, and obtaining the services of yet another superman, G E Duke, upped the record by some four miles an hour with yet another new Norton model.

With the round of continental Grands Prix that followed in that year of 'Peace in our time', 1938, the 350 racing Norton was still a force to be reckoned with, but sadly the Senior models were becoming outclassed where flat-out speed was required and the pattern was now one of making up on the corners for the speed they lacked on the straights against the might of the blown BMWs and Gileras. As one observer of the racing scene had remarked in *Motor Cycling*: 'We must produce supercharged 'Multis' for racing NOW' But Norton policy was one of no change.

If we forget the certain beatings now being experienced abroad, there was much to take place at Donington Park. Towards the autumn months of 1938 the Dunlop Jubilee Meeting was held, with flags, bunting and much celebration – certainly more continental than anything experienced on the mainland before in association with motorcycle racing; indeed it took on more the complexion of the TT races. All the big names in the industry converged on the place, while the programme listed some of the finest racing motorcyclists ever, a truly exciting atmosphere. The works Nortons took care of the main 350 and 500cc events, in the capable hands of Messrs Daniell, White and Frith with

Mr Horton gaining victory in the sidecar races. A pleasing interlude came in the programme when it was announced that Harold Daniell was to make an attack on the existing lap record, riding his alcohol-fuelled Norton. With the track all to himself, he set off on a couple of warming-up laps, and with a serious third proceeded to knock several seconds off the 500cc record and indeed the 1,000cc record to boot – registering a new time for the near three-mile circuit of two minutes, twenty-five point two seconds, a speed of nearly seventy-five miles per hour. The only sad moment on that remarkable day was when a certain young man lost a brand new Parker pipe. In the International Six Days Trial, neglected rather in these pages in favour of Norton racing successes, the Royal Army Service Corps and RAC teams were mounted on International Models, both competing for the Nazi Minister of Sport's special prize – The Huhnlein Trophy: swastika armbands everywhere, but British riders felt reluctant to raise their right arms in the fascist salute. An uneasy feeling was in the air, and yet one final year of those remarkable 'thirties was nearly at its birth.

Eight months of peace remained, and the amateur speedman's prayer was answered. The Norton spring-heel frame was at last made generally available to riders of either the two 'Inters' or the ES2 at the greatly reduced price of £7.10.0. Now young Bob, who lived up the hill at the Old Rectory, his hair immaculately greased, arranged his scarf, zipped up his brown suede windcheater, checked that his plus-fours were hanging evenly, then swung aboard the waiting 500 Inter; spring wheel, racey tanks and dull-plated Brooklands can; and rode to 'call on the girl I love' – glorious days, alas now gone for ever.

On all the road models Nortons now included electric lighting and horn in the net price; previously they had been optional extras.

Larger saddles were fitted to all machines, and a fully cylindrical silencer. The front brakes were now mounted on the offside of the hubs, giving a more direct and effective control and facilitating the fitting of a speedometer drive. The highly 'seductive' three-and-a-half gallon International petrol tank could be fitted to the push-rod operated overhead-valve ES2, at an extra charge of £1.10.0.

The exterior engine parts were highly polished, instead of the original

sand-blast finish, and all models except the Inters were equipped with quickly detachable and interchangeable wheels. On the overhead-valve engines the whole of the valve gear was enclosed and the valve rockers were carried in a single aluminium casting, with a six point fixing to the cylinder head.

There was no question of the telescopic forks being made available to the general Norton owner, they were really still much in an experimental stage, but the girder forks of Norton manufacture, in addition to the natural central spring, were also fitted with the additional

One of the highlights of the Dunlop Jubilee Meeting at Donington. Daniell, on a dope-fuelled Norton, raises the lap record to near 75mph

check springs, one on either side of the forks at their uppermost ends.

To prevent Old Jones having to have an operation which he certainly could not afford, a prop-stand was fitted in addition to the front and rear stands. Pillion foot-rest lugs completed the list.

Again the Trials specification was available on any model for an extra five pounds. The cheapest model in the range was the 16H, priced at £61.5.0, and the most expensive and sophisticated 500cc International at exactly £100.

A twelve model programme for 1939, with the two, now veteran, side-valves, the 16H and Big Four still providing

'roast beef' qualities for heavy side car work. The 600 overhead-valve Model 19 was another old favourite, ideally suited for fast sidecar or solo use. Models 50, 55 – 18 and 20, the former two machines being single- and twin-port 350s with overhead-valves; the latter two being 500 versions of the 350s. While finally came the rorty stuff in the shape of the 500 overhead-valve ES2 (the most popular machine with the sporty type who could not afford a 'Cammy' model), the camshaft models CS1 and CJ, 500cc and 350cc respectively, and the two 'Inters' Model 30 – 500cc and 40 – 350cc. 'A machine to suit all

tastes and all pockets', how rarely, if ever does one hear that said today?

And so to the last pre-war season. Nortons had decided not to race officially as they were heavily committed with manufacture of military models, but plans were made to enter the previous year's Manx machines. Finally it was decided that the 1938 TT bikes should be made available to Daniell and Frith, and although not on record as being so, John White certainly rode a Norton which had every appearance of 'factory' about it. In the Senior TT the Nortons, sadly beaten by the blown BMWs of Georg Meier and Jock West,

Donington again, venue for the speed tests of the International Six Days Trial. Competing for the Huhnlein Trophy are RAC riders Middleton, Southall and Lucas on their 'Inters'

carried small auxiliary petrol tanks in addition to the main one to ensure that the previous year's occurrence, when only the smell of the fuel remained in the tanks at the finish of the race, was not repeated. In all fairness it must be appreciated that the non-supercharged Norton was capable of about 120mph, but the German BMWs by the very fact they were employing a system of forced induction were at least 26mph faster. It is creditable therefore that Freddie Frith piloted his Norton into third place behind the German machines at a speed that was approximately but two miles per hour slower. Less than twenty-four hours prior to the writing of these very lines the writer sampled a very fast three-cylinder two-stroke from the Orient. Here was a machine that once warmed up sufficiently would go straight

through its five-speed gearbox to 120mph. Perhaps a younger man will take this all for granted, even being a little blasé and with a bare tolerance for the men and machines of pre-war days. There are others however who will hold in even greater respect those men and machines of yesterday.

It would be so pleasing to conclude this last pre-war chapter and write glowingly of continued Norton racing success, vanquishing all opposition, but it was not so. In the Junior TT Harold Daniell had admittedly finished only eight seconds behind Velocette-mounted Stanley Woods, and had at least ousted the screaming DKW two-stroke, brilliantly ridden by Heiner Fleischman, from second place.

In the Ulster Grand Prix, later in the year, Freddie Frith would describe how when in the lead on his Norton, chin jammed well into the tank top pad, feet on the rearward footrests, elbows in, and doing everything to urge the bike along, Dorio Serafini on the blown Gilera Rondine drew alongside, gave Freddie a friendly grin, took a large handful of twist grip and disappeared into the blue

We were being beaten, and that was that. Had Nortons given greater heed to the utterings of those who knew that multi-cylinder racing models were the only answer for success, in the earlier years, the late 'thirties scene would no doubt have been very different. A purely personal view of the situation is that had James Norton lived a further twenty years, he would certainly have ·required no prompting to get a 'multi', racing under the Norton banner. The magic had gone however for Nortons, a sad farewell to the Golden 'Thirties.

IN SERVICE DRESS

An overhead–valve Norton fulfils a
military role in 1941

Just how many Norton machines were produced for war service is not known with complete accuracy, but it certainly was in the thousands. The chapter is a short one, for although one cannot lightly dismiss the brilliant service the machines gave, the standard War Department model remained very much the same throughout its period with the Services, and that was all about it.

Bracebridge Street supplied nearly exclusively the Models 16H and Big Four side-valve machines to War Department specification, production having commenced during 1939.

In nearly every theatre of war, the good old Norton side-valvers were to be found, the Model 16H more often in solo form, while the larger 'Big Four' was hitched to a form of sidecar. Most motorcycle manufacturers were supplying machines to the forces, overhead-valve models finding favour with the dispatch rider, but the rugged 16H Norton with its basic simplicity, was also a favourite where quick servicing was needed. Colour finishes varied according to the particular service in which the machines were employed, for instance, the two shades of blue according to Air Force or Navy use, and olive green for the Army. Many will recall the service 16H, looking very basic in appearance with not a spit of plating and the exhaust system matt finish. Large pannier carriers were placed on either side of the machine at the rear and the most robust of folding prop-stands with its pivoted foot were very obvious features. A large unit number was stencilled in white on either side of the tank while both the twist grip and dummy grip were covered in strong webbing. Many will also recall occasions when the Allied Forces were ordered into quick retreat, and where no time existed for slightly crippled Nortons to be taken also; the British Tommy took his rifle butt to the stout cylinder to prevent Jerry from making use of the machine.

The Big Four as previously mentioned was used in sidecar form, although it would be absurd to describe the attached 'chariot' as a sidecar in the proper sense. The larger 633cc model was in appearance very similar to the 16H, but that 'sidecar' was a very spartan device consisting of a metal platform, and a front shield curving upwards and slightly backwards with a hand-rail at the top. Amidships was a metal pan seat, and a spare wheel was set across the rear of the contrivance on a suitable 'A' type bracket. The complete outfit was designed with the idea of transporting troops in twos or threes quickly to places inaccessible by other types of vehicle although often a rig or tripod

was attached to the forward part of the 'sidecar' on which was mounted a Lewis or Bren gun, not unlike the Motor Machine Gun Corps of the First World War.

A unique part of these Big Four outfits was the sidecar wheel-drive which could be brought into operation as and when necessary. The driver operated a lever on the nearside of the machine which, if pulled in a particular direction, would engage the rear wheel spindle by a system of dogs to a live axle through to the sidecar wheel. Naturally it was necessary to come to a halt before the assembly could be either engaged or disengaged, although at very slow speeds it was just possible with a well-timed pull to effect the

Sir Archibald Sinclair, Secretary of State for Air, inspects an armed Big Four outfit, used by the Home Guard during the very early 1940s

operation in the hands of an understanding 'Squaddy'.

There will be many happy memories and perhaps others not quite so happy, for those that sat astride a service Norton during those war years. Perhaps a brief respite from the wretched enmity between so-called civilised nations were the number of Service Trials that were held between 1939 and 1945 where the massive Norton could be seen thumping its way over rocky terrain and through muddy streams. In desert lands the ever ingenious DRs now in khaki drill would 'breathe' upon their service model for a little bit of high speed nonsense in the sand. Ever optimists, letters poured into the offices of the motorcycling journals from servicemen all over the world, suggesting how they would wish their peacetime Norton to be. In 1946, for those that happily returned, some of their wishes were granted.

SECOND PHOENIX

The postwar ES 2, now with
telescopic forks

At the end of August 1945 Norton Motors Ltd, were released from their war-time contract and by September of the same year the old favourites, the Models 16H and overhead valve 18, were again available at £99.0.0 plus £25.8.2 purchase tax, and £105.0.0 plus £26.19.0 purchase tax respectively. These first post-war models were still virtually in their pre-war guise, retaining the girder pattern fork and solid rear frame. These were years of great austerity when push-bikes and motor cars were still very drab in appearance, the former with their all black finish and wooden pedals, it was certainly quite remarkable therefore that the two Nortons had chromium plating both on their tanks and wheel rims.

Road racing on the mainland was being organised once again, at least as far as the paper work was concerned, but sadly Brooklands Track was finished for the enthusiast, sold to Vickers Armstrong for £330,000. Additionally Donington Park was not available,

however this was the period of the mushroom short circuits and there were to be plenty of them.

Such a British institution as Norton Motors nearly possessed a strong continental influence in these early post-war years, for there was talk of the machines being produced under licence in Spain for the Spaniards who demanded a really sound machine but were not allowed to spend their money outside their country.

By 1947 Nortons announced their ten machine programme, and all the old models, with the exception of the two 350s 50 and 55 and 600cc model 19. At last telescopic forks (no doubt as a result of severe Army tests of such forks during the latter part of the war) with hydraulic damping were standard on all models, but the plunger rear suspension was fitted only to the ES2 and all camshaft machines. The old 'cammy' models CJ and SC1 became the Internationals, while the production racing machines a few of which had already been raced in the 1946 Manx Grand Prix, were listed as the 40M (350cc) and 30M (500cc) – The Manx Norton.

Two new machines to the range were both Trials mounts in 350 and 500cc capacities. Joe Craig, who had left Bracebridge Street for work elsewhere, during the war years now began his happy re-association with Norton as their technical director, and things got back into their old stride.

With very little time for any serious development work, the TT machines for 1947 were basically the 1938 works models with very slight modifications, and with the restriction of Pool petrol, Craig suffered more than one headache in his attempt to obtain the necessary power and performance from motors previously tuned for the petrol/benzole brew, in fact the Norton Wizard was heard to remark on one occasion 'I did not think Pool was so vicious as it is'.

The old magic was returning however, although under a special ruling both supercharging and the entry of

Above : To be known as the 500T, a super trials mount, virtually a sophisticated Model ES 2 without rear suspension. Below : President of the Board of Trade Harold Wilson (later Premier of Britain) engaged in conversation with Jack Williams about the latter's ISDT Inter/Manx model at the Earls Court Show, 1948

Above : The International, more beautiful than ever. Below : Speed king
John Cobb returns from a run on Artie Bell's 1948 Senior TT winning Norton.
Standing behind HOP 225 is Joe Craig ; Arthur Bourne, then editor of The
Motor Cycle, is removing his cap

large capacity machines from the factories of our former enemies were not permitted in international races as yet, Norton machines in the hands of Harold Daniell, Artie Bell, Ernie Lyons, Johnny Locket, Bill Doran and Jock Weddell and perhaps even Uncle Tom Cobley were being sent out to carry on winning, as they did at home and abroad, with TT wins on the basically pre-war bikes (both classes) from 1947

A star from the beginning, Geoff Duke brings his privately owned 350 Manx model across the line at Haddenham, April 1949

to 1949 inclusive.

In this penultimate year of the decade Nortons were everywhere in the sporting field, and in a new class of racing first staged in 1947 held during TT week, a race for clubmen riding virtually their road machines were let loose around the mountain circuit, and the International Norton appeared to be the machine for the job. With its full suspension, overhead camshaft motor it was a natural choice for the clubman, one particular rider by the name of G E Duke excelling in these races, and winning the Senior Manx Grand Prix also on a Norton, later in the year.

Eric Oliver, possibly one of the greatest sidecar stars ever, with passenger Denis Jenkinson (well known now in motoring circles) scooped the European Sidecar Championship with his famous 596cc Norton Watsonian outfit. In the racing-car world with the newly introduced Formula Three category (500cc) every successful car was powered by the camshaft Norton engine.

The private owner racing Manx Nortons were real beauties and were now of the twin overhead camshaft type (affectionately referred to as 'double knockers') and their conical wheel-hubs were of light alloy.

For so many years Norton had relied upon the comparatively slow-revving single-cylinder layout for all their machines, but now there came upon the scene a twin-cylinder model, soon to become known as the Dominator Model 7. Framewise, it followed normal Norton practice but the power unit was of the now very popular 360-degree side by side vertical twin. The capacity was 497cc with overhead-valves operated by push-rods which in turn were set in motion by a single chain-driven camshaft situated in the crankcase. The push-rods passing through a tunnel

in the cast-iron cylinder-block. Plain big ends were employed and the crankshaft was of the bolted-up design while the connecting rods were of light alloy. What was the reasoning behind this departure from the set Norton practice of producing only high quality single-cylinder machines?

Co-designers J E Moore and Bert Hopwood, in company with development engineer Doug Hele, maintained that the twin-cylinder design gave better torque and because of its lighter reciprocating parts could be run at much higher revolutions per minute than a single-cylinder motor of the same capacity. Additionally, a twin-cylinder could pull better at lower speeds, was easier to silence, and gave better acceleration. Improved vaporisation could be obtained compared with a single-cylinder, owing to the fact that two pistons pulled, so to speak, at the same main jet, this double pulling at the jet causing a more constant depression in the carburettor.

The twin–cylinder 500cc Dominator Model 7 broke a long Norton tradition of 'one lungers'

The Dominator was an instant success although traditionalists still fiercely defended the 'single'. This brand new design from Bracebridge Street, selling at £216 including purchase tax, became the forerunner of all later Norton twin-cylinder designs. The flashy colour schemes for flashy tastes were not yet part of the motorcycling scene, and the 'Dommie' was finished in the traditional classic Norton silver-grey, black and chromium hue.

Under the chairmanship of C A Vandervell (a famous name) Norton Motors went ahead with their programme of post war models, but late in 1949 decided to cease production of their 350cc Trials machine, but the larger model the 500 T continued in its original form as an all alloy engined overhead-valve machine, fitted with Norton 'Roadholder' telescopic forks, but a solid rear end, and the pleasingly shaped alloy fuel tank. The ground clearance was considerable, and of course essential for the purpose for which it was designed. Perhaps this model, that won many trials awards, could be fairly described as basically an ES2 with certain important refine-

ments.

In the normal range of models, the plunger type rear suspension was available on all but the side valves and Model 18. On the Inters, alloy barrels and heads were now standard.

With the re-emergence of the old continental challenge (reinstated for International Racing) and indeed other British manufacturers now fielding superior raceware viz: the very fast twin-cylinder AJS Porcupine (so named because of its spiked finning on the cylinder heads of its horizontally positioned engine) for 500cc class racing, and the Velocette in the 350cc category, Nortons realised that if they were not to be caught napping then a completely new design of racing motorcycle would be necessary.

At Blandford (Dorset) road races in May 1950, the new Norton made its first official appearance with Geoffrey Duke in the saddle.

Attributed to Rex McCandless of Ireland, as designer, the frame was to become affectionately known as the 'Featherbed'; this followed a try out at Silverstone by Harold Daniell, who had remarked that the road holding

was as near perfect as could be desired, and the comfort similar to that of a feather bed.

Originally designed to house a four-cylinder unit of the 'across the frame' type so beloved of Italian race factories, the main frame was of duplex construction consisting of two long tubes approximately shaped into a trapezium and joined at the steering-head only, the horizontal tank rails at the bottom of the head and the sloping front down-tubes to the top of the head. Cross tubes were welded on at certain points, and gusset plates that served the dual purpose of rear fork location and provided attachment points for the footrests, brake pedal and gear change assembly. The rear supension was of the pivot-fork type (a proper spring frame as opposed to the earlier sprung heel) mounted on silent bloc bushes and working against coil springs which were hydraulically damped in both

Bell (left) and Duke break records at Montlhéry late in 1949. The fuel tanks possessed a striking similarity to those fitted to the later Featherbed model

The proposed Norton Four

directions. The famous Roadholder telescopic front forks were standard but the top shrouds were removed in order to permit the attachment of the two-piece handlebars which were clipped on in turn to each part of the upper fork assembly on either side of the machine. The system permitted a rider to adopt a considerably lower crouch when well down to it. The famous Norton slab-sided tank disappeared and in its place one of much simpler construction, for it no longer hung over each side of the top frame tube, but now sat on the sponge rubber-covered tank rails and was secured by a long metal strap that ran from an anchorage at the steering-head end, over the tank top, to be secured by a tension clip at the rear. The oil tank was positioned amidships underneath the rider's thighs, and the gearbox was re-designed.

Where thoughts towards multi-cylinder engines had been manifested with

The Featherbed Norton makes its first racing appearance, at Blandford Camp in 1950, with Geoff Duke aboard

production of the Dominator for road use, Nortons still pinned their faith on the well tried 'double knocker' single-cylinder design for racing purposes. It would be very interesting to learn why the policy was so, when there had been clear evidence of a four-cylinder racing engine under consideration. On a visit to MIRA test track near Nuneaton during the very early 'fifties, the author spotted a particularly fleet sidecar outfit with every indication that the motorcycle part of the set-up was Norton, with an exhaust note that clearly sung the unmistakable song of four cylinders. Local talk around the circuit on that day was that the device was very much a scaled down version of the then current BRM engine. Upon completion of several laps, the rider, possibly the late Cyril Smith, brought the outfit in, whereupon it was rapidly covered over with a large quilted waterproof sheet. That was the end of that.

The new Featherbed Nortons were not aesthetically pleasing in their original form, and in fact were a little lumpy with their 'bustle' or tail fairing that formed the streamlined continua-

tion of the one-piece racing seat. The machines were of course in an advanced experimental stage when they appeared at Blandford but, what was most important, they were far superior to their predecessors in every way and a matching force for their rivals, especially where roadholding characteristics were concerned. Absolute top speed was perhaps another question.

It could be but yesterday that listeners to the BBC radio transmission from the Isle of Man (a full half hour perhaps twice in one day) heard the late Graham Walker, affectionately referred to as the 'Glencrutchery Nightingale', describing the scene prior to the Junior TT of 1950. Walker gave details of the new Norton, and if the writer's memory has served him well, Walker's words were as follows: 'This latest Norton from Bracebridge Street is totally different from anything we have seen from that factory before, and in practice it has put in some remarkable lap times, and the latest recruit to the team is Geoffrey Duke from St Helens, from whom we expect great things'. Great things indeed,

for the Nortons swept the board in both Junior and Senior races with first, second, and third places in the two events. Duke, the gentle, handsome former Royal Signals DR, who had served his novitiate on the earlier home tuned plunger Nortons with wins in the 1949 Clubmans TT races and the Senior Manx Grand Prix event in September of that year, plus a really terrific ride, all one hundred miles of it, at Silverstone when he chased the three works AJS Porcupines home into fourth place, now as smooth as they came in his very advanced one-piece leathers, smashed Harold Daniell's 1938 race and lap record by a considerable margin in the Senior to win his first International TT race. Artie Bell and Johnny Locket were second and third in due order. No doubt riding to Joe Craig's orders, in the Junior event Bell won, Duke was second, with Harold Daniell in third place. In the Senior especially there was certainly opposition in the form of the works

Rex McCandless, designer of the new Norton frame, wheels in Artie Bell's Junior TT winning model

Above: The Featherbed Dominator, £270 worth of Norton, for export only.
Below: The veteran Joe Craig surveys his brood of Duke (centre), John Lockett (right) and Jack Brett, who came first, second and third in the Junior TT, 1951. The man in the hat is Gilbert Smith, then Norton chief

A typical private owner with his Featherbed Norton, Ken Rickard, changes gear at Beckett's Corner, Silverstone, during a 1952 meeting

Moto Guzzi, and British AJS Porcupines, for Nortons it was just like old times.

The 1950s were exciting years, in fact it is held by many that this was the greatest period in motorcycle racing history with seven or so works teams battling it out on some of the finest racing circuits in the world, dullness and procession racing was indeed a rarity. In the early years of the decade Germany fielded their much revised DKWs and BMWs (supercharging was now banned in International Races), while the Italians with their unblown four-cylinder Gileras and fantastic Moto Guzzis, later to be joined by the all conquering MVs, screamed their machines in fury against the Norton, AJS and Velocette raceware that were then so much a force to be reckoned with. As the 'fifties progressed, old names from both German and Italian factories re-entered the racing scene – indeed there was never a dull moment.

The list of post-war Norton racing successes are far too numerous to mention, the situation was just as it had been in Jimmy Guthrie's day, indeed Geoff Duke was referred to as the post-war Guthrie by many enthusiasts and admirers. The TT, Grand Prix after Grand Prix, race and lap records all falling to Joe Craig's boys on their Featherbeds – dramatic moments – witness Reg Armstrong's primary chain snapping at the very moment he crossed the finishing line to win the 1952 Senior TT.

By 1951 the private owner was able to purchase his racing Norton with the new frame, the very first production model arriving in April where it occupied pride of place in a display at the Transport and Communication Pavilion during the Festival of Britain. In outward appearance the machine was very similar to the works jobs in many ways, but it did not sport the streamlined tail. Needless to say by the time the full racing season was on a good number of these new Manx Nortons were winning races in the hands of their delighted owners, although the earlier plunger-framed models, becoming known as the 'Garden Gate' Nortons were still giving a good account of themselves in national races on the mainland.

Messrs Duke, Dale, Lockett, Cromie McCandless, and substitute Jack Brett who came into the Norton team following the enforced retirement of Artie Bell after he had received serious injuries in a continental Grand Prix, continued the score of Norton wins. Maestro Duke brought off the 'double' in the TT races and goodness knows how many events abroad.

Eric Oliver, with passenger Dobelli, slides his Norton/Watsonian outfit on the Estadio bend inside Ernesto Merlo (Gilera sidecar) in the Spanish Grand Prix, 1952

It was during the French Grand Prix that an interesting hybrid Norton was spotted in the paddock. It was a twin-cylinder Dominator unit housed in one of the Featherbed frames, and yet later a similar device was ridden in the International Six Days Trial by a British rider, R Clayton. Whether or not the two machines had any connection with Bracebridge Street as far as their construction was concerned is not known, but by the time the Earl's Court Motorcycle Show came in November, there, glistening on the Norton stand, was the Dominator DeLuxe Model 88, the first of the production Featherbed Dommies, with but one reservation, it was 'presently for export only'. Finished in polychromatic grey it was indeed a fine machine, with

its luxurious dual seat and neat little instrument panel atop the upper fork ends, although the squashed pear-type silencers and rather curiously shaped front mudguard took a little getting used to. For £270 the overseas enthusiast could be the owner of one of the most desirable road machines in being. Norton Motors presented Editor Arthur Bourne of *The Motor Cycle* with one of these models a few months later, and the writer was given the opportunity to take a short ride on it. It was an experience never to be forgotten, superior comfort to any machine I had ever previously ridden, and perfect roadholding coupled to a sweet running 500cc twin-cylinder engine. It was with some reluctance that the Norton was returned to the Paris Garden motorcycle park.

Not to be outshone, the standard road-going Nortons in the range, with the exception of the Dominator 88, now had their fuel tanks finished in enamelled silver. 'The Unapproachable Norton, Upholder of British Motor Cycle Supremacy throughout the World', so ran the advertisements, and indeed this was true, but the rumblings behind stage could not be ignored. Geoffrey Duke and company were still virtually unbeatable, and three times world sidecar champion Eric Oliver, now using the famous 500cc 'Featherbed'

Geoff Duke (seated) with Kavanagh, Armstrong and Parry. The 16-inch wheel experiment was later abandoned

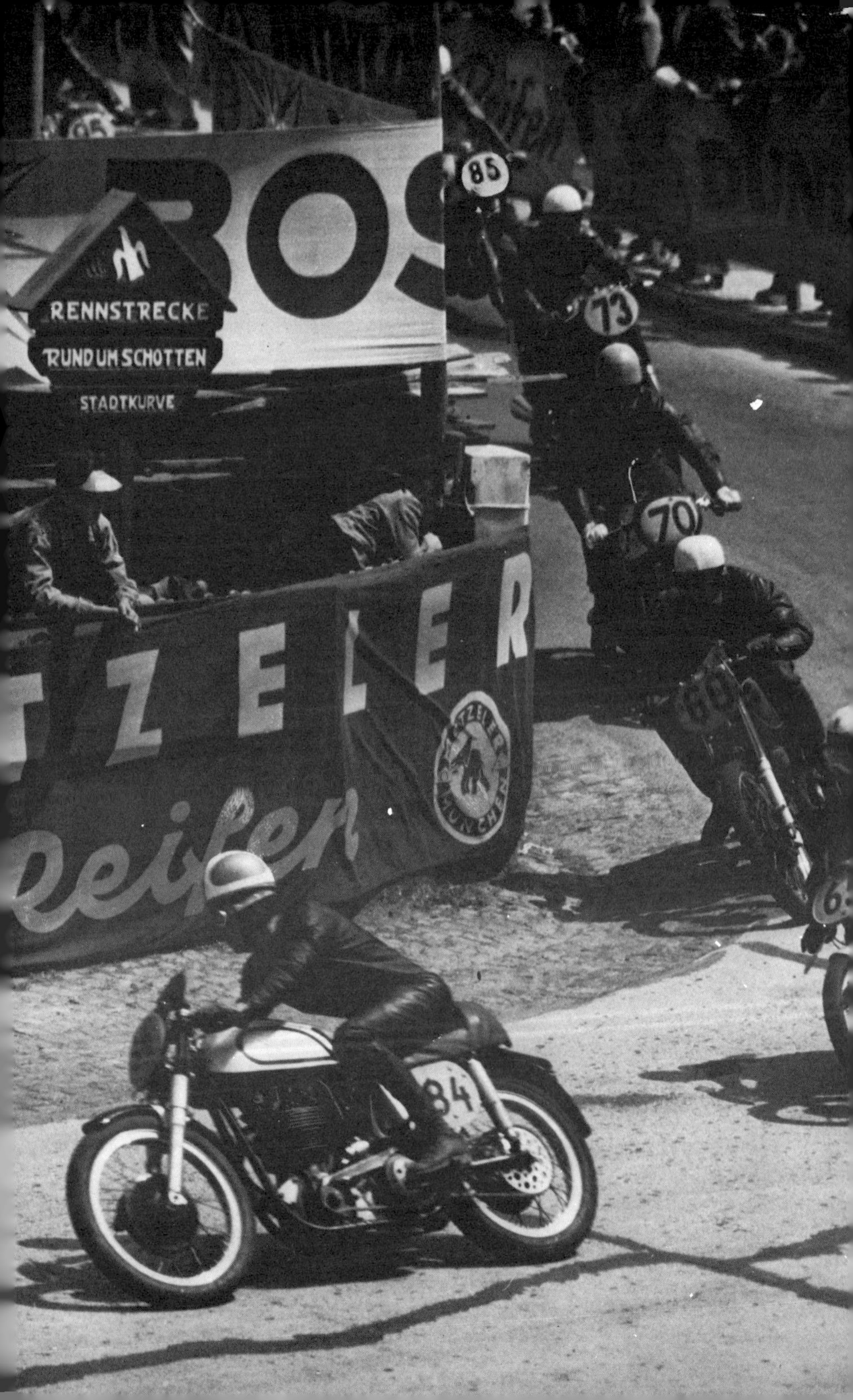
RENNSTRECKE
RUND UM SCHOTTEN
STADTKURVE

hitched to a racing Watsonian sidecar
could beat the very best of foreign
crews, but even here the German
BMWs were starting to make their
presence felt and all too soon were to
relegate to lesser placings both the
Italian Gilera outfits and the Nortons of
Oliver, Cyril Smith, Bill Boddice and
Pip Harris.

Completely to vanquish the Bracebridge models was to take some doing
however, and in 1952 modifications
were made to the official works machines, the most important being a revi-
sion of the ignition system. The punishment that the small working parts of a
magneto are required to suffer at peak
engine revs is severe. Appreciating
this only too well Nortons, in close
association with Joseph Lucas, introduced to their racing models the
rotating magnet type of magneto in
which the windings, condensor and
contact breaker assembly did not
rotate, but had the magnet rotating
about them. Such an instrument was
mechanically stronger and far better
balanced. Purely as an experiment the
works models were also fitted with a
sixteen-inch rear wheel and a four-
inch section tyre, with the TT results
again a triumph for Norton in both
bigger classes. Reg Armstrong won
the Senior event, following Geoff
Duke's retirement in the race, although
the late and sadly missed Les Graham
on his mighty MV Agusta just ousted
Ray Amm (Norton) from second place.
Duke and Armstrong were first and
second in the Junior.

Although not of the Featherbed type,
the earlier Dominator twin (standard
model) and ES2 were, during the latter
part of 1952, fitted with their own type
of pivot fork spring frame, dual seats
and the squashed-pear type of silencer,
but the enthusiast could still not get his

hands on the DeLuxe Dominator which was still for export, and selling very well abroad. The International models, still with the single overhead camshaft engine, were now of the Featherbed type and finished in the now familiar polychromatic grey. The senior model was priced at £280, while the 350cc machine was only ten pounds less.

With all the excitement and glitter, now so sadly missing from present day motorcycle shows, Geoff Duke received the Segrave Trophy for upholding British prestige before the world by winning in 1951 the Junior and Senior TTs, The Junior and Senior Belgian Grand Prix, The Senior Dutch TT, The Junior French Grand Prix, The Junior and Senior German Grand Prix, The Junior and Senior Ulster Grand Prix and the Junior Italian Grand Prix. Very succinctly, upon receiving the Trophy Duke had said, 'Looking back at the past season, irrespective of the

Veteran Stanley Woods tries the Flying Fish for size, while Ray Amm supports the tail end

type of circuit the multis have finally arrived'.

Further to pat one's patriotic back, G E Duke became the holder of the world's championship in both 350 and 500cc classes, and received an OBE for services to British motorcycling, in the New Years Honour's List.

It is a tragedy that we fell from such a mighty position in later years. And yet still not finished in 1953? Geoff Duke's words could not be taken lightly and the single-cylinder Norton was in all fairness surely becoming obsolete for big-time racing honours. Rather ironically Moto Guzzi were to enjoy some remarkable racing years with their single-cylinder design, but they had explored the sphere of super streamlining coupled to extreme light weight and this development subsequently proved highly successful. Nortons were not slow to investigate the possibilities of extensive streamlining, however, and in an effort to provide the works machines with more speed, a highly unorthodox model, for Nortons, was given a try-out in the North West

200 early in 1953, the device being appropriately called the 'Flying Fish'. The whole layout was extremely low, with the rider laying almost in the prone position; it would perhaps now be referred to as a 'kneeler'. The now famous but outdated 'double knocker' single-cylinder engine was retained in its usual vertical position, while a sponge rubber covered 'pan' was positioned over the 'works', on which the rider lay. The rear brake and gearchange mechanisms were operated by the rider's feet, although, rather than up and down movements, backwards and forwards was more the case. Light alloy panels covered the front wheel and extended rearwards to approximately amidships, and there was also more or less complete enclosure of the rear wheel. The whole thing was an interesting exercise. In the 350cc class of the early Irish classic meeting the Flying Fish completed three laps before retiring from the race, but not before it had made fastest lap. A further outing was made in practice for the TT with Ray Amm

aboard, passed by the ACU scrutineers as perfectly safe (the Norton, not Amm) it put in some tidy laps, but it did not appear in the races themselves. The conventional machines, equipped with oil-cooled exhaust valves and 19-inch rear wheels once more came to the line in both Junior and Senior events, both of which were won by Amm at record race and lap speeds. A purely personal view of those TT races in Coronation Year: they were victories more for Amm than for Norton. This very slightly built but tough little Southern Rhodesian was absolutely fearless in the saddle of his racing Nortons, indeed there are memories of him broadsliding a works Norton during a wet Isle of Man race in a way that made strong men turn away. Amm rode hard all the time, took well cal-

Dutch TT, Assen 1953. Ray Amm (17) about to leap aboard his Norton, while Duke, now riding for Gilera, is alongside. Examples of BMW, Moto-Guzzi, and AJS raceware are clearly evident

culated super risks, and could beat faster machinery to the winning post as a result. Such men are few and far between.

In the Clubman's races held during TT week, the Featherbed Internationals were represented adequately, but here again the BSA Gold Star machines were showing them the way round.

With Geoff Duke now riding for Gilera, it had to come, the opposition was more than enough for the Nortons, and the order was now one of coming through to win should an Italian machine suffer trouble when in a leading position; at least in the 500cc class. The 350cc category was still safer ground and, yet again, Junior versions of the Gilera and MV were being developed as were the most successful of all racing DKWs from Germany, the three-cylinder models, if not at that period too reliable, but considerably faster than the very best Norton.

Hopes materialise for the utility and sporting road rider at last; the Dominator DeLuxe Model 88 was made available on the home market, now fitted with light alloy cylinder heads and a more conventional front mudguard. Any patriotic race enthusiast at the 1953 Show who employed just a little imagination could well have conjured in his mind the answer to the fierce racing challenge from abroad: take a pukka works Norton, remove engine and gearbox, insert in place the four-cylinder in-line double overhead camshaft 500cc engine as exhibited on the famous JAP stand. As the

Above: The 'proboscis' Norton at Floreffe, ungainly but functional.
Right: Ron Watson (Watsonians) congratulates Eric Oliver and passenger Les Nutt on their Sidecar TT win at nearly 69mph, Clypse course

Tottenham firm's hand-out mentioned: 'This engine has been designed for Formula 3 car use, but could be developed for racing motor cycles'. One hastens to add, no disrespect to Bracebridge Street.

Undaunted, the racing Nortons were groomed for the 1954 season, the last year that the factory fielded genuine works specials. This was the year of the small outside flywheel, a design that reduced the overall height of the engine without unwanted reduction in flywheel inertia. Dispensing with internal wheels permitted the connecting-rod to be reduced in length proportionately to the shortened stroke now introduced. Streamlining of a rather ungainly type was used, in which a long proboscis aluminium

cowl extended far ahead of the steering head, while on either side of the machine faired pannier fuel tanks were placed about the position of the engine.

Though not pretty in appearance, Ray Amm once more brought this Norton home in first place in the shortened Senior TT race (the foulest weather for many a year) ahead of the Duke/Gilera combination. Both Amm and Brett retired in the Junior race, allowing commonwealth rider Rod Coleman to bring his experimental three-valve AJS through to first place. On the shorter Clypse circuit in the Isle of Man, the Sidecar TT, re-introduced after a lapse of twenty-one years gave Eric Oliver, enjoying his last year of sidecar predominance, a handsome

win over Hillebrand and Noll on their BMW outfits. Oliver's Norton/Watsonian rig being of a very advanced type for its day, a streamlined 'kneeler' – the very first.

By now it will be obvious to the reader that Norton racing successes came in cycles throughout the years of production, following a distinct pattern of glory then defeat, with the whole operation being repeated again. Many considered that Bracebridge Street was failing as a motorcycling institution,

Return of the 600 OHV Model 19 in 1955 : this is the solid frame version

when in addition to their withdrawal from entering first flight works machines in 1955, certain old favourites, plus two comparative youngsters, each in their own turn were discontinued from the standard range. Gone were the very backbone of Norton ware, the two sidevalves Model 16H and Big Four, plus the Model 18, and the real youngster, the 500T trials machine. However as if to sweeten the bitter pill the 596cc overhead valve 19 was re-introduced in both solid and spring frame versions, being considered a suitable machine for either solo or sidecar work as had been the intention

way back in the 'twenties. Light alloy cylinder heads were available on the ES2, the new Model 19 and both Dominators, the Featherbed DeLuxe version having a full width light alloy front hub as well.

Plastic tank badges appeared, and were not particularly nice, but things have since changed in this direction as we shall see.

SHOW LIST FOR THE 1955 PROGRAMME

Model	Type	Capacity	Price		
Model E S 2	OHV	500cc	£204	12	0
International	OHC	500cc	£273	12	0
International	OHC	350cc	£266	8	0
Dominator Model 7	OHV	497cc twin	£233	8	0
Dominator 88 (Featherbed Frame)	OHV	497cc twin	£259	4	0
Model 30 Manx	OHC	500cc	£465	12	0
Model 40 Manx	OHC	350cc	£465	12	0
Model 19R	OHV	596cc	£190	16	0
Model 19S	OHV	596cc	£208	4	0

AGAINST THE TIDE

One of the last pictures of Joe
Craig, steerer of Norton racing
fortunes for over a quarter of a
century

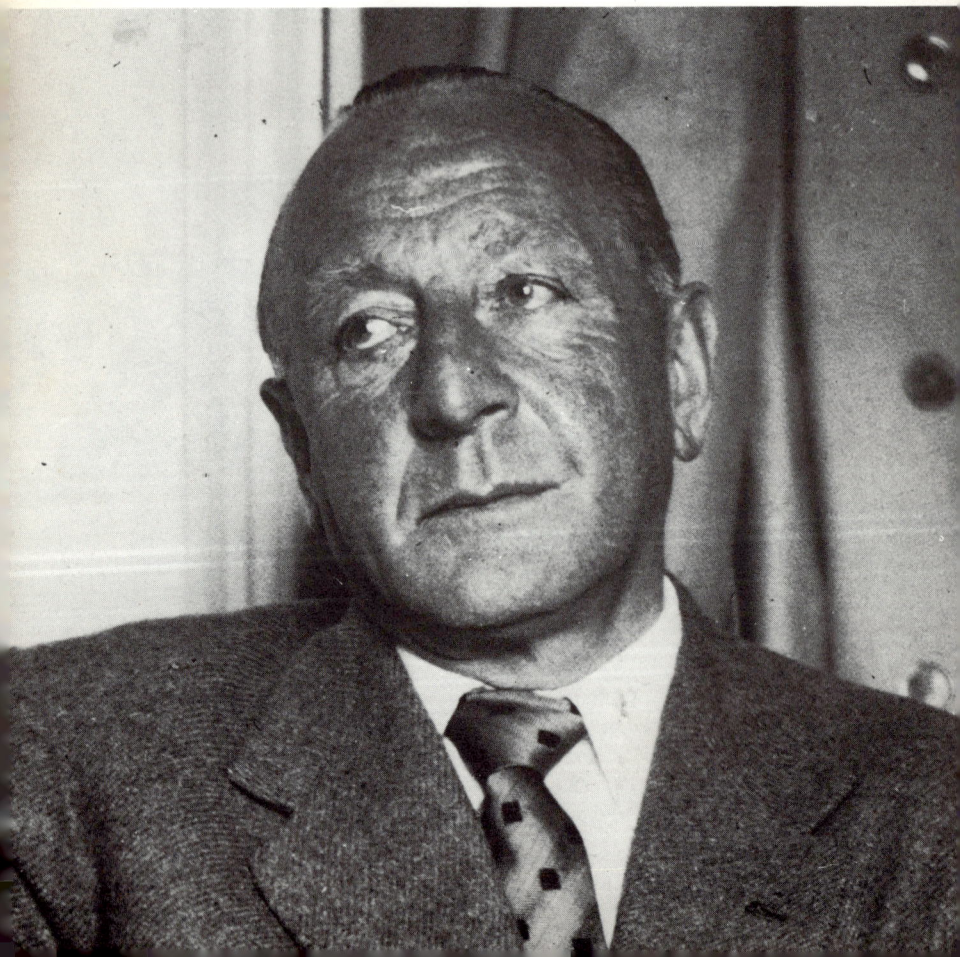

Rather like a candle when nearing its end; the flame flickers with an intense brightness for a few moments before the inevitable extinction. The Norton's end was a similar experience. Because of the rising costs of building and maintaining works specials, the factory entered all the major road races with machines much more on a par with the private owner Manx models, with riders of the calibre of John Surtees, Bob McIntyre, Jack Brett and John Hartle as team members. In most cases the Nortons were raced 'naked' as opposed to the full 'dustbin' fairing sported on the continental raceware of the period. It was not until 1961, however, that a Norton was again to win an international TT in both Junior and Senior classes, when Mike Hailwood took his single-cylinder model, tuned by Bill Lacey, round the Isle of Man course at over 100mph to secure a 500cc victory. Bob McIntyre was second on a similar model while third-place man, Australian Tom Phillis, rode a works-prepared 500cc overhead-valve twin, based on the Dominator Roadster, with a lower built version of the famous Featherbed frame. The machine was something of a rush job; nevertheless Phillis also lapped at over 100mph. Meanwhile Phil Read had won the Junior event on the Monday, forcing his Norton to a win at over 95mph.

Hailwood's achievement was an historical landmark for Nortons, being the first occasion on which a single-cylinder machine of any kind had lapped the classic course, and finished, at a three-figure speed. One must not be allowed to forget however that it was to Derek Minter's credit that the very first over-the-ton lap had been achieved, his Lancefield-tuned Norton retiring from the race on the third lap of the 1960 Senior TT.

Precipitating the introduction of Tom Phillis's 'Domiracer', back in 1955, Reg Dearden of Manchester, one of the most loyal Norton patriots and private entrants had entered in the Senior TT a modified Dominator 88

fitted with high compression pistons, megaphone exhausts, high-lift cams and revised rocker gear; its appearance was very businesslike indeed.

1955, and Eric Oliver, 'Duke of the sidecar World', retired after twenty-five years of racing. The motorcycle Press's appreciation ran as follows: 'Oliver's name first reached the headlines in 1947 when he was uncrowned King of Cadwell Park, and driving his outfit rather in the style of a Bucko Mate dealing with the crew of an old time Hell Ship. His methods were crude but they got results. Many prophesied the most gruesome end for him unless his tactics changed. But finesse was quickly acquired and in 1948 Oliver took his outfit abroad to pit his skill against the cream of continental talent'.

Many would say, and indeed correctly, 'A sidecar race without Eric was like a kiss without a moustache'.

Towards the end of the year the Model 50 (350cc) was re-introduced and a 600cc version of the Dominator 88, the Model 99, appeared, while the earlier Dominator Number 7 with the standard frame was discontinued. Finishes were in black and silver enamel for the single-cylinder range, and polychromatic grey for the twins. The Model 19 was now available with a spring frame only.

Finally, 'Mr Norton' himself, the mighty Joe Craig, retired from Bracebridge Street. This was the man who had raced so successfully himself during the early 'Twenties, both in his native Ireland and in the Isle of Man on the old Norton flat-tankers. The most patient of men, with an inherent and considerable engineering skill, and yet with not one letter following his name: the man that had steered the Norton's fortunes through the late 'Twenties, the remarkable 'Thirties, and early post-war periods: the severe disciplinarian who never quite forgave anyone who dropped one of his precious racing machines. Alan Wilson, who had been competitions manager at Bracebridge Street, now became manager of factory road racing following Joe's departure. Somehow things would never be the same again.

In 1956 John Surtees joined MV, but John Hartle won the Senior class of the Ulster Grand Prix on a Norton machine. A newcomer to the standard range was the Model 77, a 600cc twin, but with the standard type of spring frame. Finished in polychromatic grey, the 77 was intended mainly for sidecar work. Squashed-pear silencers were out, and new tubular ones in. The new twin sold at £260-8s. At that year's Motorcycle Show Norton single-cylinder models sported pushrod upper tunnels cast in the cylinder head. New front hubs and brake plates could also be seen.

In March 1957 Joe Craig was killed in a motor accident near his home at Landeck in West Austria, aged fifty-nine. AC generators and coil ignition were seen on Duplex-frame Dominators for the first time that year. Nortons did well in the 1957 Manx Grand Prix.

In 1958 C Gilbert Smith gave up his position as managing director of Norton and its R T Shelley subsidiary, after forty-two years association with the famous marque, from office boy to managing director. A well known talent spotter for potential works riders, Gilbert Smith used to upset James Norton by preparing his own trials machine during business hours. Slazengers racing team (Nortons) included Alan Trow, Jack Brett and Michael O'Rourke.

The range of Nortons for 1957 ran as follows: Model 50 ES 2, 19S 77, 88 99 40 and 30 Inters and 40 and 30 Manx. For 'desert going' there was an adaptation of Model 77 (600cc) for competition riding in the United States, first of the trial bikes. Model 77 had clipped mudguards, 'sit-up-and-beg' handle-bars and two-into-one exhaust pipe on the right hand side.

Geoff Duke was riding his own

1959 version of the model 50 350cc now in an all welded Featherbed frame. The bulge on the forward end of the primary chain case houses the AC generator

private Nortons, but he also had works rides on BMWs.

Mike Hailwood made his presence felt on Nortons at Brands Hatch in May of 1958. Norton sidecar ace Eric Oliver came out of retirement and rode a 497cc Model 88 Dominator hitched to a Watsonian Monaco chassis-less sports touring sidecar in the Sidecar TT: an exercise to demonstrate the capabilities of a roadster outfit with only a certain amount of engine modification and tuning. Former lady road racer Mrs Pat Wise was Oliver's passenger and was not required to perform any of the usual sidecar acrobatics. Although in Oliver's estimation he was giving away at least 40mph to the BMW outfits the Norton finished in tenth place. Models 50 and ES 2 were produced in all-welded Featherbed frame, further, both singles were featured with crankshaft-mounted AC generators.

International models were discontinued, and also the Model 19S which had served so well as a sidecar machine and fast solo bike. The 'haulier' capabilities now came within the realm of the standard roadsters, any of which were available with the special sidecar fork rake, trail dimensions and gear ratios. All single-cylinder models in the range came in Forest Green, plus the usual chromiumplate, although listed as an extra, the 50 and ES2 could be obtained in the more traditional black and silver colour scheme. The twins, Models 88 and 99, could be supplied with twin monobloc carburettors, polished ports and large inlet valves as extras, with red, blue or black and silver finishes. All models had an enclosed rear chain.

An introduction dating from that year was the overhead-valve 250cc model designed by Bert Hopwood. The frame consisted of a pressed steel front down tube member. Twin top tubes ran horizontally beneath the fuel tank and dual seat, to the rear wheel, where they supported a well styled rear enclosure. Charcoal Grey and Mountain Rose were the colours of the two-tone

A new Bracebridge Street product. The twin-cylinder 250cc Jubilee model, designed by Bert Hopwood

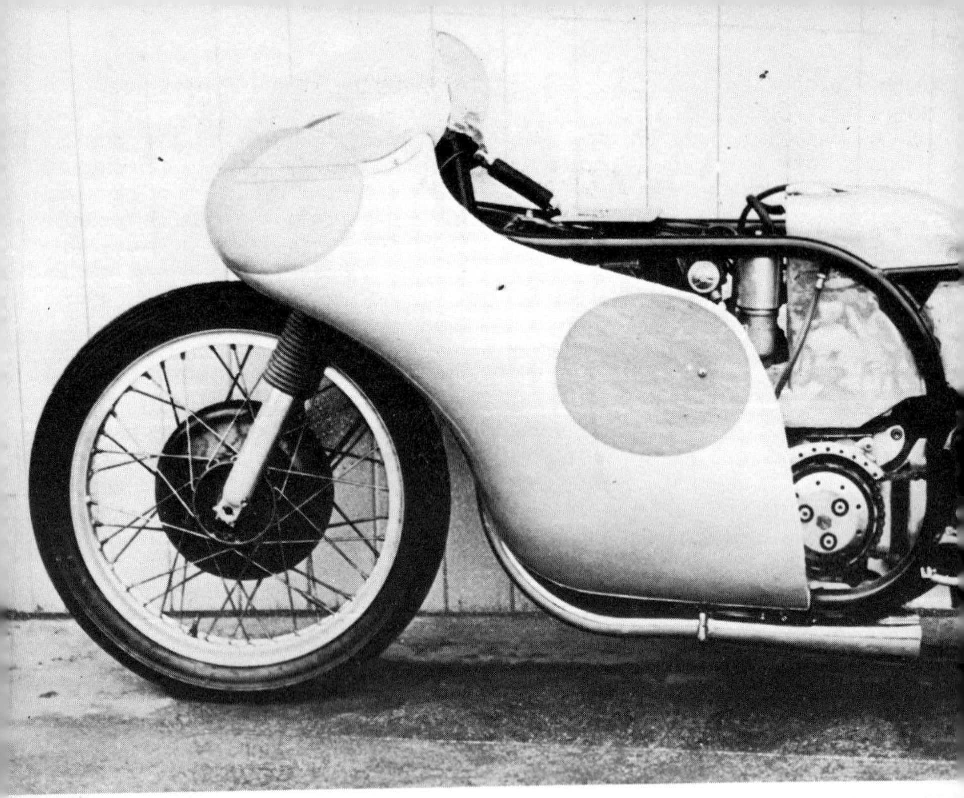

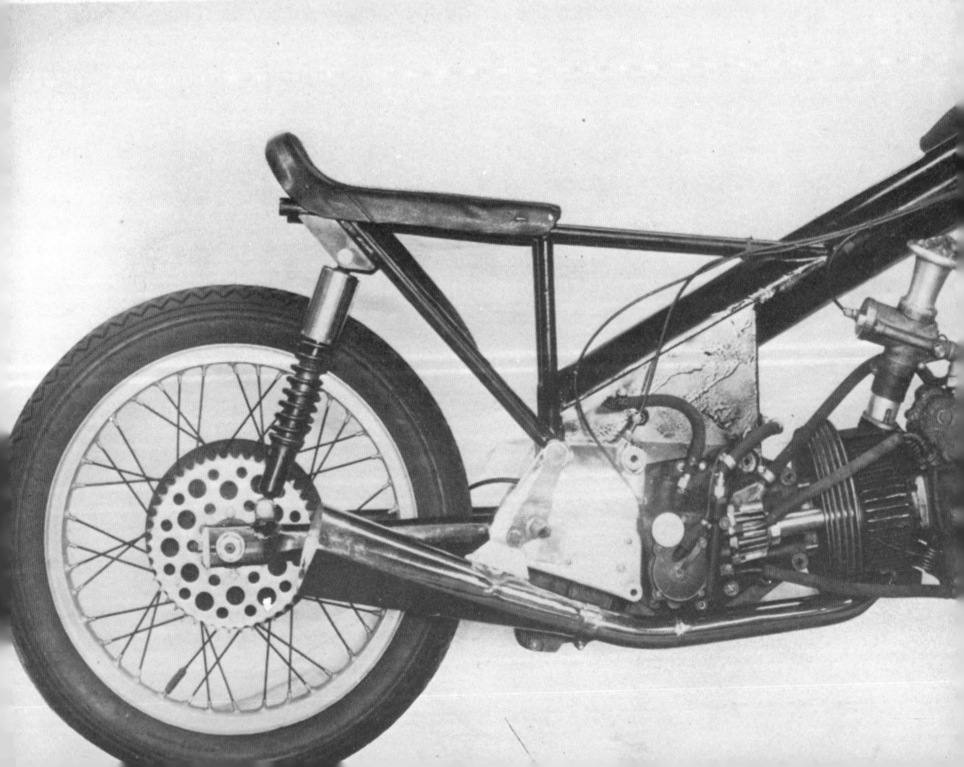

finish. The price was £215-16s-4d, including purchase tax.

At the 1958 Motorcycle Show the Dominator Model 99 was presented in blue enamel finish. The Nomad, twin-cylinder 600cc had the earlier type of spring frame, available for overseas markets only. The show range comprised: Jubilee 250; Model 50 (350); Model ES 2 (500); Dominators 88 and 99 (500 and 600cc respectively); Manx Models 40M (350) and 30M (500), both priced at £496-10s-1d.

In 1959 Rem Fowler at last received the Hele Shaw Trophy for his twin-cylinder Norton win in the 1907 TT! By some curious set of circumstances it was not presented at the time of his victory. Rear enclosure appeared on Model 99 Dominator DeLuxe; the Nomad was still for export. The late Gary Hocking entered in major road races on Reg Dearden's Manx Nortons in this year. Neat Royal Automobile Club's box carriers in fibreglass were attached to ES2 Nortons.

1960, and a DeLuxe Dominator 88 was among the year's models. Geoff Duke retired from racing motorcycles, Derek Minter won the 500cc class of the North-West 200 on his Norton, and up and coming rider Phil Read made good headway on Norton machines. Not enjoying retirement from the cut and thrust of racing, Eric Oliver decided to have yet another ride in the Sidecar TT. Oliver had built a very streamlined Norton Manx model and Watsonian sidecar, with standard gearbox shell and five-speed internals supplied by Harold Daniell. The very experienced Stanley Dibben was passenger. Oliver was also down to ride in the 350cc event on a Manx machine. A severe prang in practice on the outfit put him out of both races, and he was in plaster and back on the mainland

Horizontal engine position as Moto-Guzzi, an experiment born in 1955

before he knew what had happened.

An experimental Junior Norton was used in practice for the TT with former Manx Grand Prix winner Eddie Crooks in the saddle. The machine was a very much lower Featherbed, with the fuel tank under the rider's seat, whilst the exhaust pipe passed underneath the engine with the megaphone directly facing the rear wheel. The Press was told in 1960 that a horizontally placed engine was envisioned. Hailwood came third in the Senior TT, his Norton following two works MVs home. Phil Read won the 1960 Senior Manx Grand Prix. The narrow Featherbed frame was introduced for single-cylinder Nortons. The upper rearward runs of the main loops were narrowed so that with a narrower nose dual seat a more comfortable riding position was provided (the previous year's Manx frames were such).

Men who made Norton history in the 1960s. Stan Hailwood (centre), his son Mike (left) and Derek Minter. Both younger men had lapped the TT course at over 100mph on their single-cylinder Nortons

The Jubilee 250 was to be called the Jubilee DeLuxe, a standard model without the tail assembly was to be introduced. Mike Hailwood made the first lap at Silverstone at over 100mph by a motorcycle on his Senior Norton. There was the Manxman Model, twin-cylinder 650cc, with high handlebars and a standard frame, for the American market. 1960 also saw the first appearance of a 350cc version of the Jubilee, called the Navigator. Norton offered the technical editor of *Motor Cycle* magazine a 'Jubilee' for his return to London from Birmingham. Vic Willoughby was amazed at the machine's terrific amount of urge. Norton later confessed that it was in fact the new 350cc Navigator. Navigator Standard cost £229-15s without tail; Navigator DeLuxe, with tail, cost £237-12s-7d. Both cylinders, on the Jubilees and the Navigators, were cast singly.

In 1961 came the Dominator Sports Special, in both 500 and 600cc forms; the Dominator 88 Sports Special and Dominator 99 Sports Special respectively; both models had two-into-one exhaust systems, and twin carburettors,

and were designed for production racing classes.

Bert Hopwood went to Triumph and Alec Skinner took over the position as managing director of Norton Motors Limited. For TT practice Doug Hele, as development engineer, introduced a Dominator-engined Manx model, but the frame was some thirty to forty pounds lighter than the standard Manx one. 1961 was also a year of certain experiments in the Norton racing department.

Nortons once again, after some years, won both bigger classes of the TT races, referred to a little earlier in detail. The Sports Dominators excelled in the big 500-mile production races on the mainland, and John Cooper entered the racing scene on Nortons.

Even bigger Dominators became available. The 650cc Model could be had in standard, DeLuxe and Super Sports versions. R N W Holmes, well known correspondent in the letters columns of the various motorcycle journals, built his ideal machine; the old 16H side-valve unit in a Featherbed frame.

With 1962 came the Atlas Model 750cc

twin, a machine developed from the 650 Dominator, but with a standard frame, and high 'cow horn' handlebars. It was for export only, however. The Silverstone 1,000km production race was won by Phil Read and Brian Setchell on a 650cc Sports Special Norton, with a further win for the trio in the Thruxton 500-mile event.

Doug Hele went to Triumph; he resigned from Nortons following the announcement that the Bracebridge Street works was closing and moving to London. Eric Oliver was sprinting at Ramsgate with a supercharged 500cc Dominator and Watsonian racing sidecar.

In 1963 the 500 and 650cc Dominator twins were listed in Standard and Sports versions only; dropped was the Model 99 600cc range – reasonably since the 650 had so much more power for only 50cc more. The remaining models in the range consisted of the two singles, Models 50 and ES 2. The 250 Jubilee in two versions, and likewise for the 350 Navigators. Many

The Dominator Sports Special, supplied for production racing, 1961

Above : The old Model 50 in its new livery, catalogued as the Matchless G 3.
Below : Bill Stuart, master of Norton racing engines

Above: One of the last Manx Nortons. Below: The Manx engine, the world's most famous single-cylinder racing unit

different colour schemes were available, but the 650cc Sports Specials, the only models to have magneto ignition, were finished in black, silver and chrome.

Nortons were now being built at the AMC works at Plumstead, South-East London. Made to special order for the American market certain 350cc Navigators were, in 1963, blown out to 400cc, equipped with electric starters, and named the Electra; later, these were made available to home buyers, classified as Model ES 400. Rem Fowler, winner of the first TT twin-cylinder class, died, aged 80.

Production ceased of single-cylinder

roadsters, while the twin-cylinder range was re-tailored; accordingly the smaller models were available in touring guise only, and the larger ones strictly in sports trim. The 750cc Atlas continued for export only, more or less a Norton engine in a Matchless (AMC) frame.

The greatest blow was still to fall, for by October 1963 production ceased on one of the most famous racing motorcycles of all time, the Manx Norton. Sadly, space prevents a due appreciation of such fantastic machines. Fortunately the complete stock of spares, tools and special jigs was purchased by Colin Seeley, who continued to give service to the Manx owner, until he in turn sold out to John Tickle of Huntingdonshire, who is

Police mobile, 1967, with specially equipped 650cc Sports Norton

determined not to allow the demise of the models, now called the Manx T5.

In 1964 the Norton Atlas became available for British enthusiasts at last, but fitted with Featherbed frame, twelve-volt electrics, roadholder forks, eight-inch diameter front brake and twin monobloc carburettors. A very handsome machine, this, with its chromium mudguards and silver-grey petrol tank; it was priced at £359. The compression ratio was on the low side, at 7.6 to 1, but it gave the engine greater flexibility in spite 'of its shattering acceleration. To achieve this, the piston crowns were concave.

A Norton advertisement for 1964 read: 'Norton Dominator 650 Sports Special – 12 Months Guarantee – plus the name on the tank'.

It is at this point that the AMC influence was very apparent on the 'Nortons', firstly the famous old models, the 50 and ES 2, passed from the range, strangely to be re-introduced as the Matchless G3 and G80 respectively, but with Norton badges on their tanks. They were listed primarily to meet the demands of the export market. The transitional period was a rather complex one, and by the end of 1964 the Norton list ran as follows: Jubilee 249 twin; the Model 50 Mk 11 (Matchless G3); the Navigator 349 twin; the ES 400 twin; the ES 2 Mk 11 (Matchless G80); the Dominator 88S, the Dominator 650 Sports Special and the Atlas 750.

Hardly had the programme been set, when the 350cc Navigator was dropped, the reason given being that: 'The fewer the differences, the lower the level of production costs'. By comparison with Norton policy in the earlier years the whole matter was most unsettling.

1965 passed as a comparatively peaceful year without any major changes and Joe Dunphy riding his Manx model finished second in the Senior TT behind Mike Hailwood on the 'Fire Engine' MV, a similar state of affairs to the previous year's event when Derek Minter had performed the 'Dunphy'.

The experts and the bowler hats were much in evidence at the AMC factory in Woolwich towards the end of 1966, and the outcome of their visits was reported in the motor-cycling Press as follows: 'Production is again in full swing at the AMC factory following the acquisition by Villiers, who have obtained the rights to manufacture AMC machines. Five famous makes have been saved from extinction by a deal between the AMC receiver, appointed last month, and Manganese Bronze Holdings Limited, of which Villiers are a subsidiary (an answer to the author's reference to all being quiet on the Woolwich Front during 1965).

'All five marques; AJS, Matchless, Francis Barnet, James, and Norton, are being continued, and the Woolwich factory will remain in operation for at least a year. The name of the new company will be Norton Matchless, Ltd.'

Some of the 'famous names' were, however, to fade from the scene in due course. The proof of this lay in the fact that no new models appeared on the road from at least three of the marques. On the strictly Norton side of affairs, all the smaller capacity models were dropped, and in one instance the Atlas engine found itself housed in a standard AMC frame. The famous Featherbed frame was set aside solely for the Dominator 650 Special Sports, and the 750cc Atlas machine with two-way progressively damped Roadholder forks and full width alloy hubs.

In comparing the Atlas and 650cc engines, the only external difference was the breather pipe from the camshaft tunnel on the larger capacity unit, but as a whole the two machines could be readily distinguished by the Cherry Red petrol tank on the Atlas, compared with the silver tank on the 650 SS.

Things had got a lot worse before getting better, but now at last it could be seen that the Norton Phoenix was nearing its regeneration.

THE RENAISSANCE

The earliest Commando in frosted
silver finish, sensation of the 1967
Motor Cycle Show

It was in the Spring of 1969 that the writer saw his first Norton Commando, parked just off Marylebone High Street in New Cavendish Street. Having despaired of the tragic efforts made by some manufacturers to produce a decent motorcycle after the late 1950s, I had lost interest in other than a few dated thoroughbreds and would not have turned twice to view the pathetic machinery that now 'graced' the scene. Being a very hard man to please when motorcycles are under 'scrutiny', the Norton Villiers Company may take it as the supreme compliment that I spent the best part of an hour being seduced by that Commando,

just two years ago. It is into the age of Aquarius that we are now entering, the astrologists tell us, a period in which technology and all that is associated with it shall play a major part in our mode of living. It would appear that the Norton Villiers Company are projecting this conception in the production of a quite revolutionary motorcycle, revolutionary at least in comparison with other makes.

Such thoughts are furthered, when, in 1967, under a new engineering director, Dr Stefan Bauer, then based at Wolverhampton, the Commando started to take shape. It is hoped that the good doctor will not take offence, but one's thoughts do tend to turn to a scene of clicking computers, and a white-coated Dr Bauer, gazing intently over his rimless spectacles.

One imagines that the Commando was the end product of much research, and earlier development work on the large Norton vertical twins, especially the Atlas model, although there had been talk of an 800cc twin, with unit construction, and double overhead camshafts driven by chains running through tubes like short pushrod tunnels. Additionally there might have been a five-speed gearbox, the entire assembly being housed in a Featherbed frame. Perhaps the Commando was a compromise between the Atlas and the rumoured twin?

The original 750cc twin-cylinder Commando was a machine of very advanced design; perhaps one should say 'is of very advanced design', for this book has been written just four years after the model was born; now comes the appropriate moment to fall into the present tense, at least for a description of the machine.

The styling is very modern, but tasteful, especially the Fastback model, whereas other versions are needed to satisfy the young man who still has to express himself in more demonstrative ways. The motorcycling Press commented: 'On looks alone the new Norton Commando would be outstanding in any company, for this is far from just another version of the familiar Atlas'.

The fuel tank, dual seat and tail fairing are styled to form a three-piece unit and so give the model distinctive lines; the cylinders are inclined forward, the gearbox is close to the crankcase to form a compact assembly, and there is a new primary chain case (enclosing a triplex chain) with single bolt fixing. The engine is rubber (Isolastic) mounted, following automobile practice, which, in concert with the frame design, is covered by patent.

The frame is quite unlike the Featherbed version, but equally interesting in concept and construction. It is light but possesses tremendous strength. The main member is a very large thinwall tube ($2\frac{1}{2}$-inches in diameter) braced to the steering head. A duplex cradle in one-inch diameter tubing runs from the steering head to loop under the power unit and rises to points beneath the seat struts from the top tube to form a triangulated structure with the rear members of the cradle loops. Claimed advantage of the design is that all the stresses are taken by the top tube and rear triangulations, the cradle being merely an engine mounting convenience. The forward part of the top tube is subject to bending only, while the struts are in direct tension or compression, and so give resistance to twisting.

Very unusually, the rear fork is not pivoted from the frame, instead the pivot is carried by the engine plates. Engine, gearbox and rear fork in turn form an independent sub-assembly, carried at front and rear in outsized rubber bush mountings. The mountings allow the sub-assembly a degree of shock absorbing movement in longitudinal or vertical planes but prevent lateral and twisting motion.

The engine unit is of course the 745cc Norton Atlas, but embodies improvements to crankcase pressure release valve and timed breather. New-type pistons provide a compression ratio of 8.7 to 1 as compared with the previous 7.6 to 1. A welcome item is the Lucas 12-volt Zener diode system, plus capacitor ignition which permits the machine to be run, if required, with the battery removed.

Carburation is provided by twin Amal concentric units coupled to a large capacity still air chamber and induction silencer. Front forks are the famous Norton Roadholders, and an eight-inch diameter two leading shoe front brake is a standard fitting. The fuel tank, of three and a quarter gallons capacity, is in fibreglass with a snap action filler. Also of fibreglass is the tail piece which embodies the rear lamp and registration plate, and includes space for the tool kit. The front mudguard is of light alloy.

The original finish of the Commando was all silver, giving it a somewhat Teutonic appearance, with a choice of dual seat colours. Present models are supplied in various colours, although the Commando that the writer saw back in 1969 in London, had the familiar green tank and tail piece assembly; incidentally, there exists no such colour as British Racing Green.

Production racing that really took on during the early and mid-'Sixties seemed to favour the big capacity Nortons, and with the further introduction of a production TT race in the Isle of Man in 1967 a Commando model was entered. Regrettably there followed a subsequent withdrawal from the event as riders Peter Inchley and Ron Chandler were refused an extra practice period by the ACU, following slight troubles with ignition, brakes and suspension during the official practice period. However, good things were to come.

At the Earl's Court Motor Cycle Show, the Commando was the talk of the place, for it represented a new concept in motorcycle design and construction, and a stirring force from the peculiar apathy that had set in with the British motorcycle industry. It started to make the motorcycling public feel patriotic once more to home-produced models, and in fact has continued to do so. Great credit must go to former Grand Prix driver Dennis Poore, chairman of Norton Villiers, whose dynamic determination to put the Commando on top, has proved so very successful.

Some confusion exists as to when the Woolwich works finally closed, for although an announcement appeared in the Press in January 1968 stating that Norton had closed the South London factory, a further announcement was made some seventeen months later advising readers that at this period the last machine left the Woolwich works. Regardless of this little complexity however by April 1968 the first batch of 750cc Norton Commandos were due to roll off the production line in a new factory adjacent to the Midlands, accompanied by the slogan 'It's Britain's fastest, smoothest and dearest bike' to which a motorcyling Press tester added 'Probably the most dangerous aspect of the Commando is starting it, a kick back from this one is likely to send you into orbit'.

Although the Commando was the leading protagonist of the Norton range, the 650cc Sports Special with its Featherbed frame became the Mercury Model, a single-carburettor, 47bhp machine giving Norton Big Twin acceleration speed, steering and roadholding for less than £400 (actually it was £388-0s-1d).

The Atlas model passed from the range in its original guise, while the standard (Matchless) framed P11A 750cc became known as the Ranger, for road or rough stuff use. Rather pleasingly, the old Norton policy came to the fore once again, for after a Commando had won the 750cc Production TT in 1968, and was the holder of the one-hour speed record for 750cc motorcycles, plus being the fastest road motorcycle, having cov-

Freddie Frith, OBE, Norton star of the 1930s, astride one of the earlier Commandos, with Norton-Villiers Chairman Dennis Poore

COMMANDO
750 S

ered 126.7 miles in one hour. Norton advised in advertisement form that here was a machine 'The same as you can buy'.

Voted by the readers of *Motor Cycle News* no less than three times Motorcycle of The Year, the Norton Commando may well add a fourth title before this year of 1971 is through, an exciting state of affairs, in that the average motorcyclist, caring not so much for the country of origin, but more for the quality of the machine has voted in favour of Japanese models in previous years, to a degree. One awaits with eagerness therefore the outcome of votes cast in the Motor Cycle Election for this year.

In March 1969 slight changes were made in the Norton programme; one very simple, but none the less very important one, was the re-introduction of the proper Norton motif on the tanks of the models. There had been the stage when plastic tank badges were all the rage, and no doubt appealed to many, but they were really very cheap and nasty and destroyed a certain dignity of the motorcycle. To see once again the famous name Norton written in black on the Commando Tanks was a tonic.

The original Commando became known as the Fastback Model, while the old Ranger with its former standard Matchless-type frame was transformed into the Commando 'S' and referred to as an American-style Street Scrambler, with its high level exhaust system which gave it a generous power boost at mid-range engine speeds, and a 1.5bhp increase over the Commando Fastback at maximum rpm. The Mercury Model was continued in its Featherbed frame form.

To the writer, brought up in a period

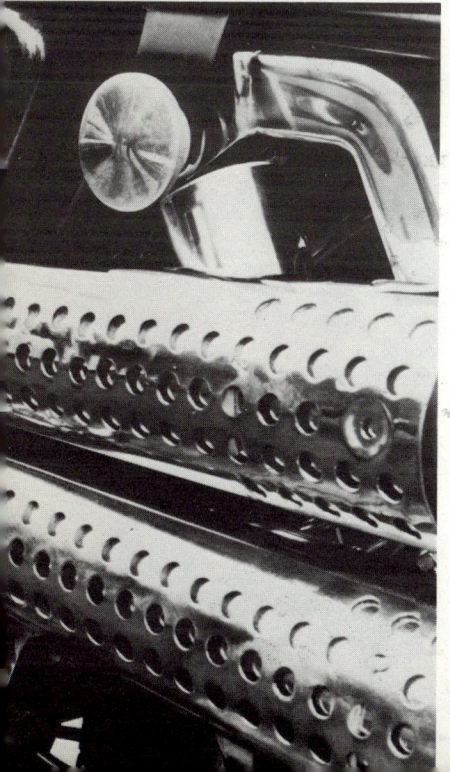

Power was boosted on the Commando S by the high level exhaust system

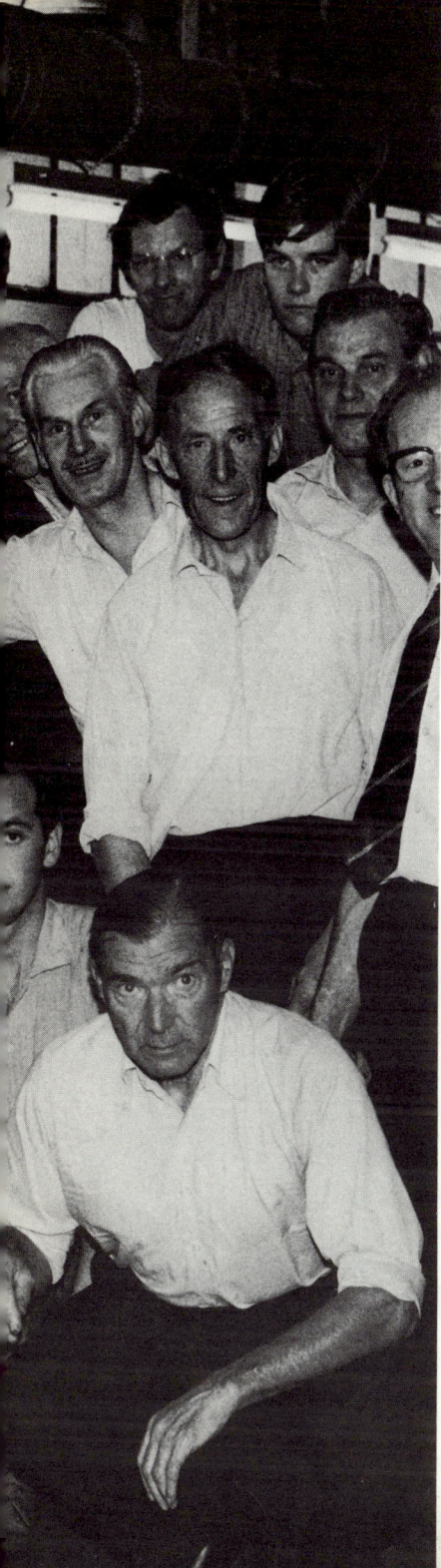

The last Norton made at Woolwich, in 1969, with some of the staff

when Norton machines were more basic in appearance, and seemed to embody Henry Ford's dictum that any model could be supplied in any colour as long as it was black and silver, the new Norton Villiers colour schemes much confused me. For the record however the 1969 Nortons could be supplied in the following hue: the Commando 'S' in either red or blue, but four different colour schemes were available for the Fast-backs viz: Grenadier Red, Green, and Quicksilver were offered on the models for the home market, while export buyers could choose a two-tone scheme consisting of Quicksilver and Grena-dier Red, the Quicksilver being similar to the metalflake type finishes so popular in America. In July 1969 it was officially announced that all Norton production would take place at the company's new factory at Andover, in Hampshire, but the engines were to be built at the engine division of Norton Villiers at Wolverhampton. The And-over premises, conveniently near to the Thruxton racing circuit for testing purposes, is Britain's newest motor-cycle factory, originally occupying an area of 25,000 square feet. Thirty Nortons were produced daily in 1969, but as Dennis Poore said at that time: 'Output will rise dramatically when a sister building of equal size is com-pleted this month (December 1969), and the factory will be making 10,000 machines a year by 1971', Poore added, 'We shall have the capacity to produce 20,000 units annually'.

The first Commando models to leave the new factory were a batch of machines called the Interpol, basically a standard job incorporating special equipment for Police work, it was possibly this order that came from the Sussex Constabulary, the complete value of the 750cc twins being in the region of £9,000.

On a hot Saturday evening last year (1970) in the Isle of Man, racegoers

155

Above: The Hi-Rider, 1971 motorcycle styling. Below: The fully race-kitted Commando, similar to Peter Williams's TT Model

Above : The 1971 fastback Commando. Below : Norton-Villiers testers stand behind variations of the Commando at the new Andover factory, January 1971

witnessed the remarkable ride by well known road racer and Norton Villiers performance shop chief draughtsman, thirty year old Peter Williams. On a fully race-kitted Commando Williams finished in second place, only 2.6 seconds behind winner Malcolm Uphill on his three-cylinder Triumph Trident, in the 750cc Production TT. The event is gaining in popularity, for there is not such a marked difference between the models raced and those used by the utilitarian rider, although replicas of William's machine are available to special order

The latest racing Norton following its brilliant debut at Crystal Palace

at about £800. And so to the last Motor Cycle Show in London held during the opening months of this year at Olympia. Five models constitute the Norton Villiers programme for 1971, machines that are all variations of the Commando, ranging from the classic Fastback to sports models and even a semi-chopper referred to as the 'High Rider', the last named being rather surprisingly, the most expensive, excluding the non-listed production racer, at £627-6s-3d.

Just when it looked as though we were to rest contentedly upon our laurels with the introduction of Production class racing as being the grandest thing we ever had done for

some years, and to my mind a sorry situation, the first seeds of a possible return to full Grand Prix racing were observed at the Easter Monday meeting at The Crystal Palace. Norton Villiers, own Peter Williams appeared on what may be described as an out and out racer from the Andover factory. A William's brainchild, the machine bears little or no resemblance to the Commando model, at least framewise, indeed the patented rubber mounted twin-cylinder 750cc engine unit is housed on the more orthodox lines, although the cylinders are still inclined forward.

While viewing the experimental Norton in the Paddock, I must confess

I was most favourably impressed; it appeared light and low, and extremely compact, in fact a very businesslike job. In the actual races for which the model was entered it really was a 'Flyer' and had it not been for slight overgearing I am sure this Norton would have beaten the Gus Khun Norton Commando ridden so expertly by Charles Sanby, as it was, following some really spirited riding, Peter Williams chased Sanby home in second place.

There now exists a Formula 750cc TT race, and Williams, riding the experimental Norton, rode brilliantly into third place, behind two three-cylinder Triumphs in the 1971 series, with a race average speed of 101.22 mph. Later in the week, mounted on a production Commando, Williams retired in the 750cc Production TT with electrical trouble, but not before he had put in what was to be the record lap at 101.06mph.

The conclusion to this book must be as follows. No British Grand Prix racing motorcycle has beaten the mighty combination of Giacomo Agostini and his 500cc MV from Italy, in the great international races over a period of some years. If the 500cc class is to remain, and there appears no move to presently change the order of things, then it would sound logical for Nortons to develop their own 500cc Grand Prix model in order to stem this continental dominance. One must realistically view the situation and accept that should MV decide to develop their own Formula 750cc Grand Prix motorcycle, could we find ourselves in such a comfortable position?

One cannot speak too highly of the patriotic efforts made by the Norton Villiers Company to put back the sting into big time racing, and it is earnestly hoped that many years hence the possibly yet unborn writer will be able to record in his own saga of such a famous marque the spirit rousing words. 'They raced from victory to victory, with almost monotonous regularity'.

American and British Usage

Variations in terms: US given first

displacement : engine capacity

fender : mudguard/wing

gasoline : petrol

gear shift : gear change

hood : bonnet

kerosene : paraffin

muffler : silencer

parking brake : handbrake

parking lights : side lights

rumble seat : dicky seat

sedan : saloon

shift down (or up) : change down (or up)

sidewalk : pavement

station wagon : estate car/shooting brake

top : hood

town car : coupe de ville/sedanca de ville

tread : track

two-cycle : two stroke

trunk : boot

windshield : windscreen

Equivalent measurements

1 US gallon = .833 Imperial (British) gallon, 1 Imp gal = 1.2 US gals ; the same ratios apply to pints.
For most purposes the US ton = 2,000 lbs. Brit ton = 2,240 lbs ; similarly, the US cwt = 100 lbs. Brit cwt = 112 lbs.
Cubic capacity (approx) : 100 cu/ins = 1,640cc, 100cc = 6.1 cu/ins.